CHANGES

**Other books by Soozi Holbeche
published by Piatkus**

The Power of Gems and Crystals
The Power of Your Dreams
Journeys through Time

Soozi Holbeche

CHANGES

A GUIDE TO PERSONAL
TRANSFORMATION
AND NEW WAYS OF
LIVING IN THE NEXT
MILLENNIUM

PIATKUS

With love

for Beinsa Douna, Brother Boris and Brother Krum, Big Maria, Marta
and Joanna, Helene, Danielle, Darinka, Jana, and everyone working for
change in Eastern Europe. With love to all who are pushed to the edge
and awaken to change. With especial love and appreciation to Desmond
who, despite his scepticism, encourages me anyway.

And

in memory of Andre Thomas who
died in 1997 before his own book
could be written.

This edition first published in 1997 by
Judy Piatkus (Publishers) Ltd of
5 Windmill Street, London W1P 1HF

First edition originally published in 1993
as *Awakening to Change* and reprinted in 1994

A catalogue record for this book is
available from the British Library

ISBN 0-7499-1763-6

The extract from *The Sleep of Prisoners*
is reproduced by permission of
Oxford University Press

Set in 10.5/12.5 pt Sabon
by Phoenix Photosetting, Chatham, Kent
Printed in Great Britain by
Biddles Ltd, Guildford and Kings Lynn

This book is dedicated to Mother Teresa and Princess Diana whose lives were great examples of the power of change through love.

Come to the edge, he said.
They said: We are afraid.
Come to the edge, he said.
They came.
He pushed them . . . and they flew.

GUILLAUME APOLLINAIRE

CONTENTS

Part Three: The Magic of Creative Living

INTRODUCTION TO THE NEW EDITION

Since I wrote the original version of this book in 1993, the world has gone through enormous changes on all levels. Ethnic massacres, torture and starvation of thousands of people, wars, earthquakes, cyclones, political scandals, aeroplane crashes, bombings, UFO sightings, BSE (mad cow disease), life-threatening viruses that do not respond to antibiotic treatment, have all contributed to a new global awareness. Threats to survival force us all to question the meaning of life.

Magazines and newspapers increasingly focus on unusual phenomena, from global patterns of weather change, the appearance worldwide of crop circles, the Photon belt (discovered by satellite in 1961) and its possible effect on our lives, to the men and women who claim abduction by aliens, and the conspiracy theories that government and big business hide much information about what is really happening from the public at large. Bestselling books exhort us to take charge of our lives in all areas of health, money, relationships and work.

Global communication via television, telephone, radio, internet and satellite gives us instant information on events that occur thousands of miles away. Surgeons have virtually mastered the art of transplanting organs and limbs. Satellites in outer space reveal that planets such as Mars may indeed have supported not just life, but a highly advanced civilisation. New ways to treat cancer and Aids, non-toxic means of boosting the immune system, and herbs and vitamins to stimulate mind power and memory, as well as prevention against Alzheimer's and senility, super-learning, speed reading, subliminal messages that affect our behaviour from over-eating to the prevention of shoplifting, hypnosis and music played before and during surgery, are no longer pie-in-the-sky ideas. Ozone and oxygen therapy, regression into past lives, acupuncture and deep relaxation techniques are amongst myriad 'alternative' solutions to curing illness, popular with both medical doctors and their patients. 'Vibratory' or 'energy' medicine is the key phrase of healers today and will be the major means to keep healthy in the next millennium, with the advantage of no toxic side-effects.

Parallel with all the transformational discoveries and inventions, we have also dehumanised life and made it needlessly competitive. We have destroyed nature, hunted animals to the point of extinction, relied on material success and possessions as a sign of a good life, instead of developing an inner state of peace and well-being. The result is that life is deeply unsatisfying for most people. We have separated our hearts from our brains, cut ourselves off from contact with the earth and nature to the point that depression, leading to suicide, has become a worldwide epidemic. A recent study of 33 countries by the World Health Organisation showed that, after violence and car accidents, suicide was the third highest cause of teenage deaths.

Now scientists have discovered that the sun as well as the Earth is changing. The 1994 Ulysses probe showed that the sun was losing its magnetic field or polarity, and was causing solar flares to increase. When these flares erupt, vast magnetic storms rage, changing the earth's magnetic fields. According to research done by Sheila Ostrander and Lynn Schroeder, authors of *Cosmic Memory*, these changes produce abnormal behaviour in humans and animals. Apparently when solar flares occur, they stimulate old emotions, grudges, fears and memory loss, and retard reactions to what is going on around us. Dr Alexander Chijevski, the father of Soviet cosmobiology, said political upheaval is facilitated when the sun rages. His research showed that revolutions, wars, political unrest, vast migrations and outbreaks of disease all appeared to correlate with sunspot cycles.

Geophysicists have told us that the centre of the Earth is crystalline in structure. Its inner and outer cores rotate at different speeds and generate magnetic fields. In 1994 a fragment of 'something' from Jupiter fell towards the earth, breaking into twenty-one fragments as it did so. As the Earth's magnetic fields were hit by these fragments, the resultant shock waves or vibrations triggered enormous unconscious emotional reactions in countless numbers of people on Earth. In other words, scientists can now explain why everyone, whether emotionally, physically or mentally, feels that 'something is happening'.

As these transformational energies affect our physical bodies and every particle of life on Earth, how can we cope? I believe the answer is to move from will-power to soul-power. To align with our own divinity – inner wisdom, higher or soul self – gives an inner security which is unshakeable, no matter what erupts around us. The key to this alignment is self-love, self-acceptance and non-judgement. Judgement usually comes from the ego. Love of self leads to unconditional love of others. (e.g. I accept you as you are and not as I would like you to be) and ultimately to enlightenment. We also need to keep our own vibrational frequencies at a high level. As we open our hearts, drop our ego-centred desires and ideas, release our emotional baggage and expand our awareness, we automatically raise our vibrations.

This book is intended as a simple practical handbook of how to assist this transformation. All the exercises in the book are self-explanatory and easy to follow. I have used them many times in the last thirty years, in individual sessions and in groups. Use them, and allow yourself to move forward. Let understanding give you power.

Part One

AWAKENING
TO CHANGE

1

GATEWAY
TO THE FUTURE

We are living in challenging times. According to historians, scientists, psychics, visionaries, environmentalists and indigenous peoples worldwide, it will be the most radical, dramatic and potent period of change in the planet's history. Almost everything we have known, valued and held on to is falling away to give birth to a new phase in human evolution as great as if we had stepped from water to land for the very first time. We are becoming part of a new species and a new culture.

The native American Indian Cherokee prophecies say that we are entering the ninth and final state of purification in which our consciousness must be transformed. In the process everything previously hidden must come to the surface.

The Mayan calendar also predicted that the years from 1987 to 2011 are and will be a time of purification. Edgar Cayce, known as the Sleeping Prophet and one of the world's greatest psychics, said in the 1930s, 'the transition will begin in those periods between 1958 and 1998. When this period has been accomplished then the New Era, the New Age, is to begin.' He added, 'Will you have a part in it or will you let it pass by and merely be a hanger-on?'

The 1990s are the gateway to the last phase of our present history. On every level huge changes are taking place which push us to move beyond the limitations of mass-conditioning, selfishness, greed and competitiveness into an awareness of other worlds and our connection to them. A massive shift that will, in the future, make even the Industrial Revolution look small, is waking us from self to cosmic consciousness.

A dream of happiness

An aspect of this shift was foreshadowed in the 1960s when the catch-phrase of flower-power hippies was, 'All you need is love.' That brief period of idealism in the 1960s symbolised a dream of happiness, fulfilment and sharing; a world where communities lived co-operatively; where nature and civilisation supported one another and where soul purpose and spiritual awareness prevailed. For many it was a new way forward, a Renaissance similar to that of the fifteenth century which resulted in an amazing burst of creative energy and a profound change in consciousness. For others it was a reactionary escape from materialism and a leap into the shimmery, illusory glamour of psychicness; with the abnegation of personal responsibility that came from following a guru and doing exactly what he or she said – whether it was to wear purple, pink or orange clothes, become vegetarian or eat meat, shave heads or grow flowing, shoulder-length hair.

It was all part of a spiritual explosion, but many outsiders reacted with fear and disapproval.

Although not a hippie, I remember being involved with a community in America which was based around our mutual commitment to God, serving the planet as best as we knew how at the time and growing a garden.

Around this time Jim Jones and his followers in the remote jungles of Guyana all committed suicide. We had never even heard of him but from that time on we were considered to be a fanatical sect. Local churches preached about how evil we were and one Saturday morning a police car roared up and seized a two-year-old baby boy who was running around naked while his father watered the garden. We were accused of lewd, obscene behaviour and sexual deviation. Accusations were levelled at us from people who, despite many invitations to do so, never came to see for themselves what we were doing. Painting, building, planting trees, digging trenches, preparing the way for a bio-dynamic garden, we were far too busy and tired even to think of cavorting naked under the trees.

Their blind bigotry was similar to those people who would not look through Galileo's telescopes in case they had to admit that Copernicus was right when he said he could prove the Earth moved around the sun instead of the sun revolving around the Earth. Many people today have exactly the same resistance to change.

The guru teachers

The 1960s and 1970s were very much the time of following the guru who could astral travel, pop into your room and take you on amazing out-of-body journeys, encourage you to explore sexuality on the understanding that unfulfilled desires would hold you back in the next life, or tap you with a feather to raise your kundalini and reach enlightenment. No wonder many students became entranced – a guru who can pop into your room and read your mind, appear and disappear through closed windows, doors or walls is more interesting than the college professor stuck in his study with his books.

The guru-teacher was right for a certain stage of evolution. However, they nearly all taught that the most important teacher we can have is ourselves; the most valuable lesson we can learn is to go within.

In 1929 Krishnamurti, the man who was believed by the Theosophists to be the Avatar or world spiritual teacher, shocked his followers when he dissolved the 'Order of the Star', the organisation established to present him to the world. He challenged his listeners to awaken to the truth within themselves, independent of any spiritual teacher or organisation.

Before Yogananda died he said it was now the end of the age of the guru and the time of fellowship. In the 1970s many teachers severed what were often emotionally addictive ties between themselves and their chelas, or students, by manifesting symptoms of imbalance and craziness.

In Australia a teacher appeared on stage with a brown paper bag completely enveloping his head. Turning his back on the audience and speaking through the paper bag, he said his vibrations were far too sensitive to expose them and proceeded to give his lecture, oblivious to the fact that three-quarters of his audience had left.

In South Africa another well-known seminar leader sat in front of a large group of enthusiastic followers with a bottle of whisky in one hand and a large can of sardines on his head. Helping himself to generous slurps from the bottle he spent three hours 'channelling the spirit of the sardines' (to say nothing of the spirit of the whisky).

Sexual scandals, bizarre behaviour rationalised as teaching devices, alcoholism, drug addiction, psychological exploitation, misuse of money and abuse of power – not just by charismatic New Age leaders but also by the Church and famous tele-evangelists – made big headlines and continued to do so into the 1980s. The amazement, shock or disappointment triggered by these antics catalysed people from dependency into discrimination; from an attitude towards the teacher of 'I'll give you my life, now take care of me', into 'I'll take care of myself'.

Most of us, when we first discover books, teachings, people or philosophies which empower us to change our lives, become like the baby who grabs, swallows, tastes and touches everything he can get his hands on. The sharper, the shinier, the more glittery, the better. Finally it's all too much and he wants to throw up. So do we – and we often need the jolt from the very person who inspired and initiated us into new thoughts and behaviour to do it.

Quest for the new

The early years of what we now call the New Age (coinciding with the time of the Punk movement when people wore safety pins in noses, ears and nipples) were a release from left-over

Victorian prudery. There was a reaction to established institutions, to the floundering of the world economy and the rape of the environment. Nature began to show symptoms of toxicity but instead of paying attention most of humanity voted for more arms, bigger cars and increased factory production, and mocked the environmentalists who spoke of acid rain and the problems arising from hacking down trees and building roads through rain forests.

At the same time, many people, dissatisfied with materialism, questioning old values and seeking a spiritual meaning to life, began to see that an immense change was afoot. There was a movement away from the city towards alternative lifestyles and community living. Small groups of people with similar beliefs, interests and questions began to come together. There was a ripple of excitement that in spite of nuclear problems and ecological imbalance the world was moving into a new phase.

This new phase included the thought that human self-sufficiency was not enough. Sir George Trevelyan, regarded as the father of the New Age in Britain, described this awakening of recognition to our relationship to the whole of life as:

> ... the greatest revolution in the intellectual climate of human thought. We are discovering that this planet is not just a tiny unimportant speck in the universe, nor are we the only civilisation. This Earth is of paramount importance as a channelling point through which spiritual beings on all levels can flow and evolve. Humanity is to be seen as a great experiment of God going through the illusion of separation from the divineness and evolving self-consciousness to achieve conscious reintegration with the divine will, in free creativity, as co-creator and companion of God.

The Dalai-Lama, a spiritual and political leader and Nobel Peace Prize laureate, says: 'Everyone has the responsibility to shape the future of humanity. So let us try to contribute as much as we can. Be a good human being with a good heart. That gives you energy, peace, tranquillity and also inner strength. Simply, you see, by being a good person.'

Credo Mutwa, long known in South Africa as a Zulu Shaman, a Sanusi or holy man, now travels worldwide and speaks of ancient Zulu traditions and knowledge that he learned during his training as a healer and spiritual teacher. In doing this he has lost the respect of many who feel he has broken an oath to protect sacred and hidden Zulu lore. Credo says: 'I saw that the lore of my people was destined to die with those of us who knew it and that it would then die for ever. I gradually recognised that by breaking my oath I was doing something for my own people, preserving the eternal wisdom that had been carried down for centuries, and also doing something for mankind as a whole.'

Credo Mutwa's teaching incorporates the idea that the soul is an integral part of God. 'Our souls came into being when God created Himself. We exist because God exists and our souls are fragments of this Universal self.' He also says that the separation of science and religion has brought us to the brink of disaster today. 'I think it is high time that science is brought back into the realm of the spiritual so that it can wear the blanket and feel the caress of spirituality and have a reverence for the world and all that dwell in it.'

Credo Mutwa's basic message is that we are all one human family, both in origin and in destiny. He believes that both we and the Earth are in danger, but that the possibility of healing is as strong as that of destruction. We must recognise one another as children of the same Cosmic Father and Mother, and drop the sense of difference and fear between nationalities, cultures and languages. 'In the world,' he says, 'there is war, disease and hunger. But wait – something beautiful is beginning to happen, for in all of us there is a god trying to be born.'

American teachers such as Deepak Chopra, Louise Hay and Caroline Myss have changed our ideas about illness and introduced many ways of how we can and must take personal responsibility for our health and happiness. Robert Monroe, Raymond Moody and Dannion Brinkley have transformed our understanding of death and dying. During his latter years, Monroe developed a unique programme called 'Going Home', which teaches people who face imminent death – whether from terminal illness or old age – how to leave their bodies at will, and so overcome any fear of the act of dying.

Raymond Moody, author of *Reunions: Visionary Encounters with Departed Loved Ones* has created a facility called 'psychomanteum', which can facilitate visionary encounters with departed loved ones, thus enabling many grief-stricken people to recover and get on with their lives.

Dannion Brinkley, author of *Saved by the Light* and *At Peace in the Light*, has apparently stimulated more volunteer hospice workers than ever before in the history of the hospice movement. When I met him he described himself as having been the type of bully – both at school and as a marine – that most of us would cross the road to avoid. Struck by lightning, he had a near-death experience that changed his life. He says there are two ways to really find out who you are. Be with a person taking their first breath and a person taking their last. In his words, 'When you find someone who has nothing to give you back except love, you find yourself . . . If you want to know there is life after death, become a hospice volunteer.'

The world is now filled with wise men and women who, in the shape of healers, teachers, therapists and shamans, remind us that we are spiritual beings having a human experience and not vice versa. Through opening ourselves to love and light we can become independent and not co-dependent. Whether the message is based on ancient wisdom or newly channelled information, we are encouraged to become do-it-yourself gurus. As one perceptive individual put it: 'A true teacher is not one with the most knowledge but one who causes the most people to have knowledge. A true master is not the one with the most students but one who creates the most masters. A true leader is not the one with the most followers but one who creates the most leaders.

Findhorn: hard work and magic

The idea that Earth is a school and training ground for soul development is not new. The principle of brotherhood of man and the father/motherhood of God is common to many religions. However, few people were able to grasp the concept that brotherhood included contact with the elemental world of nature spirits.

Two people who did were Peter and Eileen Caddy, founders of the Findhorn Community in Scotland. Sacked from his job of managing the Cluny Hotel in Forres, Scotland, Peter moved his family and secretary, Dorothy Maclean, into what he believed would be the temporary accommodation of a caravan, placed on an arid strip of sand at Findhorn bay in the north of Scotland. Assuming that he would soon resolve his difficulties with the hotel owners, the family had to adjust to cramped quarters and lack of money which finally impelled them to grow their own vegetables.

These vegetables became a legend – fifty-pound cabbages, roses in the snow, enormous carrots and tomatoes out of season. Yet when the soil was tested by the British Soil Association it was pronounced mostly sand and therefore 'dead' earth in which it should have been impossible to grow anything.

Pressed to explain how they did it, Peter and Eileen described working from daily meditation and attunement to the devas – or angelic spirits – which animate the animal kingdom. During meditation Eileen also believed that she received specific guidance from God which was then acted upon by the group.

The results were virtually miraculous and led to hundreds of curious people coming to see for themselves what was going on. Many of them decided to stay and from these small beginnings the Findhorn community, now famous throughout the world, developed. Dorothy Maclean had a strong gift for devic/angelic communication herself and was as vital a part in the founding of Findhorn as were Peter and Eileen.

Many years later, at an Oneearth Conference in New Zealand, I was standing next to Dorothy when a woman rushed up to her and said, 'Quick, quick. Tell me about the Magic of Findhorn.'

Dorothy said, 'It was not magic – it was hard work.'

'No, no,' the woman replied. 'I want to know about the Magic.'

Again Dorothy repeated, 'It was not magic. It was very hard work!'

The woman recoiled, disgusted. 'You're just ordinary – I thought you were a special, magical person.' Dorothy quietly smiled and said, 'Yes, I am ordinary – and special and magic, just like you.'

All over the planet people were beginning to experiment with the magical and miraculous through meditation, mind expansion techniques and communication with higher streams of intelligence, including extra-terrestrial – as well as talking to trees, plants and machinery.

Those who thought that, by coming together in small groups, holding hands and 'letting go and letting God', it was all they had to do soon found that letting go to God was hard work, just as Dorothy Maclean said. It meant action, discipline, putting lives in order physically, emotionally, mentally and spiritually. Many groups fell by the wayside but it was still a time of spiritual awakening, a realisation that we are more than our merely physical senses and that, in the words of F. C. Happold:

A wind has blown across the world, and tremors shake its frame.
New things are struggling to their birth and nought shall be the same.
The earth is weary of its past of folly, hate and fear,
Beyond the dark and stormy sky, the dawn of God is near.

Today the work of the Findhorn Community is recognised worldwide – even by the European Community, who helped sponsor the planning and construction of an ecological sewage site that deals with all on-site waste water. Eileen Caddy's books are translated into twelve languages and people from more than seventy countries attend courses and conferences. Eileen Caddy still lives at Findhorn, Dorothy Maclean lives in North America but is a frequent visitor, while Peter Caddy died in a car accident in 1994.

To quote from a Findhorn Foundation trustees report of 31 January 1996:

The work of the Findhorn Foundation is based on the premise that for our life on Earth to continue, fundamental changes are required in the way we relate to ourselves, to other people, to the physical environment and to the spiritual dimensions of life. The Foundation is a community where our lives together demonstrate the possibility of harmonising and integrating these diverse relationships by research, by teaching, and by providing a model in developing new ways of living that address many of the problems facing humanity today.

2

EXPLOSION
OF AWARENESS

In the 1980s the winds of change blew more intensely through the world, opening previously closed windows in people's minds, blowing away the cobwebs of old thoughts, traditions and ideals. It was like switching on a light in a previously dark room where people asleep began to wake up and take a long hard look at the world around them.

The green movement initiated a new awareness into the damage we were doing to the environment. Acid rain, holes in the ozone layer, global warming, millions of trees destroyed to provide land for cattle and paper production, many animal species decimated to the point of extinction and exhaust fumes poisoning the atmosphere: all of these things shocked us into acknowledging the relationship between over-consumption and the pollution of the Earth around us. Hundreds of people responded to earthquakes, hurricanes, changing weather patterns, disease, famine and population explosion by taking steps to become self-sufficient. Alternative technology, vegetarianism, organic and bio-dynamic farming became the order of the day. Others reacted in fear, dread for the future, confusion over the complexity of the problems faced and, ignoring the screams of the Earth to make us listen, continued to pollute and rape the planet.

A polarisation began to take place between people excited and optimistic that this was a period of cleansing and an opportunity to move forward into a new era, and those fearing catastrophe and the end of the world. In the words of Sun Bear, a native American and founder of the Bear Tribe Medicine Society, whom I was fortunate to meet and spend time with:

> I see that many humans are not yet willing to make the necessary changes in themselves and their actions which could prevent the most severe consequences. They will not stop polluting, they will not stop consuming the Earth's resources as if those gifts were theirs alone; they will not stop acting towards nature and all her creatures – including other humans – as if they were only a back-drop for their activities. They simply will not learn to walk in a sacred manner on the Earth.

The Kogi Indians of Colombia, who call themselves the elder brothers of the human race, are also convinced – like most indigenous peoples – that we will soon destroy the balance of life on Earth. Kogi life revolves around Aljuna, the mother whose life force shapes the world and makes it flower. In an attempt to get us to change our ways and relate more strongly to the world of nature and spirit they say: 'Put the brakes on. That is the law of the Mother. Put the brakes on your tongue. Put the brakes on your mind, your sex. That way you may save gasoline, and your car will go a long way.'

My own quantum leap

While prophets of doom avidly read Nostradamus and predicted the imminent arrival of the Anti-Christ (someone who causes humanity harm), war and global destruction – and others forecast the rebirth of the Christ energy into the Earth and the advent of the Aquarian Age – my life was full of excitement, adventure and spiritual expansion.

I had grown up with a psychic sensitivity which enabled me to see what people thought (which often did not match what they said!). I saw past, present and future simultaneously, would say things and they happened, have conversations with invisible beings whom I could see as lines of energy, or shadowy forms like the negative of a black and white photo. I often saw through walls, ceilings, tables and chairs. So-called 'solid matter' used to disintegrate into vibrating atoms and I was aware of the consciousness or life-force in everything around me. It was like an on/off switch in my brain that could suddenly catapult me into a totally different perception of reality.

I sometimes put my hands around ailing plants or people in pain and felt an energy, a heat, pouring through me which often helped them. We all have these capacities but at that time, knowing nothing of senses beyond seeing, touching, hearing, speaking and feeling, I became a little afraid.

As a child I soon learned that these were not experiences to talk about. If I did I was accused of lying, pretending or having too vivid an imagination.

I tried to cut these inner senses off until the day that illness, accident, constant crisis and disaster impelled me to scream at God, 'The only thing that has not happened in my life is that the ceiling has not fallen on my head.' As I spoke the ceiling crumbled and fell, knocking lamps off tables and pictures from walls. In shock I asked, 'What do you want me to do?' A voice rang through the room, 'Meditate' – and so meditate I did.

Meditation transformed my life, put me in touch with a wiser, more honest part of myself that helped me to trust and use the awareness that previously seemed like a curse. Dreams, always a strong part of my life, increased in power and clarity. In one I found myself rushing through space to hang on the moon looking back at the planet (almost like Edgar Mitchell, whose vision of the Earth at the time of the moon-landing changed his life), while a voice said, 'You have to make a quantum leap in consciousness. You think you've done so before but it is nothing in comparison to what you must do in the future.'

Part of my quantum leap was to stop doing anything I did not believe in. Ideas that life was meant to consist solely of earning a living, getting married, owning a house, a car, having X amount of money in the bank, two or three weeks' holiday a year, before retirement and waiting for death, fell away. So did material possessions.

Instead of working in fashion and design I spent my time with accident victims, cancer patients and the terminally ill. I was so poor that when the soles of my shoes disintegrated and my clothes began to fall apart I was delighted to receive cast-offs from concerned friends. I learned that when you do what you believe – the word means I be-live: I live what I believe – the universe co-operates. All my needs were met.

Wanting to meet Elizabeth Kubler Ross, the well-known Swiss psychiatrist and physician, a ticket for America arrived through the post from an anonymous donor, with a small note attached saying, 'I had a feeling you'd like to go.' Secretly dreaming of Sri Lanka and the elephants of my childhood, I suddenly received a gift in the form of a five-week holiday in Sri Lanka. I saw the house where I had lived, joined the elephants for the Temple of the Tooth procession in Kandy (an annual procession in celebration of the Buddha's losing a tooth when he visited the island hundreds of years ago), and watched extraordinary acupuncture operations where, with only needles behind the ears and in between the thumbs and forefingers, a 25lb goitre was removed, a Caesarean birth and brain surgery took place. Money for an operation I needed but could not afford came literally out of the blue. A dress I'd admired appeared on my doorstep. It was almost as if I only had to think of something and it materialised.

I discovered books, magazines and organisations which helped me understand that much of what I had experienced in childhood was quite normal. An eclectic range of authors from Herman Hesse, George Gurdjieff, Suzuki, Christmas Humphreys, Alan Watts, Alice Bailey, Ram Dass, Thomas Mann, Idries Shah and many, many others, expanded my thinking. The Sufi books by Hazarat Inayat Khan became my bible. I studied astrology, numerology, the tarot and the I-Ching. I learned about Uri Geller and Matthew Manning's telekinetic powers, which attracted worldwide attention when tested by scientists, explored Kirlian photography, reincarnation, the Kabbalah, astral travel and life after death.

I felt as if I had been living in a box and suddenly the lid was removed. I jumped out into a new and wonderful world where I was surrounded by people who had made their own quantum leap into a completely new way of looking at life; people who had not only had similar experiences to mine and felt free to discuss them but who also wanted to explore them further.

The sleeping giant wakes up

As my healing practice began to develop I was invited to Australia, America, Kenya, South Africa and many European countries to give lectures and seminars. No matter where I went, whether I spent time with Western educated or indigenous people, I saw the same things happening, as if, to quote Jean Houston, 'a sleeping giant was waking up and slowly stretching in the hearts and minds of millions'. The idea of what it was to be a human being was starting to expand.

Increasingly the stereotyped male–female roles changed. Men, embodying a more feminine energy than in the past, became more willing to show their feelings. Women, flexing a few unused muscles, began to stand up, assert and express themselves in a way previously considered masculine. In fact the 1960s women's movement began with women stepping out to claim their power. Now, in the 1990s, men are stepping in to rediscover their feelings, imagination and intuition.

In an Australian magazine I read an article (by Alan Lowen) entitled *Male ego, the longest running show on the planet*. It went on to say:

> Male ego has been running the show for a long time. It really knows how to look after itself. Yet really it is nothing more than armouring. For some strange reason, I guess in order to 'civilise the world, man decided a few thousand years ago that he needed to take the controls. Something in women must have frightened him, because in the process he started to use his power to suppress the female spirit in woman, in himself and in the world. He learned to feel less

and to care less. Gradually he came to identify himself with his thickening skin, and to lose touch with the deeper mysteries of his being.

His armour protected him from himself. His hardening and deadening affected his children, passed on from generation to generation through both men and women. It is true that there are many women whose female spirit has been anaesthetised by male conditioning, including some feminists who are as oppressive as some of their male counterparts. (The same happened in the reverse under the power of the Amazonian matriarchy.)

This deadening of, and disconnection from, warmth and feeling is what enables men and women to abuse their children, violate each other or fight bloody wars based on an inflexible belief that their way is the only way and in which people are tortured to death for having a different point of view.

It is like a blindness, symbolised by a children's story I once read in which an old man is going blind and lame. He spends his days bemoaning the fact that he has three daughters instead of sons. Repeatedly he says, 'If only I had a son he would have the strength and courage to fetch the medicine to heal me from the doctor on the other side of the mountain.' Finally, after many adventures and much effort, it is the daughters who get him to walk and to see. The story reflects the blindness of the man, or male ego (which as we have seen, can affect women as much as men) who, unable to recognise the value of feeling, imagination and intuition (the three sisters), indifferent to love and compassion, trusting only left-brain logic and the idea of masculine superiority (which boils down to the ability to do rather than to be), ceases to relate to life as it is.

This refusal to see and participate in what is real around him cuts him off. He becomes an emotional cripple. The old man's revival comes through acknowledging the power of the feminine, the power of intuitive right-brain as well as left-brain thinking which, when aligned with the masculine (the daughters put on male clothing to accomplish their task), brings about healing and balance.

Another part of the story describes how the doctor's son

accompanies the third daughter, who he thinks is a boy, through the mountains when she takes the medicine back to her father. It is a journey of many days and on the way they become friends. Once home the girl takes off her disguise and instead of being shocked the doctor's son is delighted. It is a bonus to discover that his travelling companion is female. He marries her and, like all good fairy-tales, they live happily ever after.

As the patriarchal domination of the world comes to an end, and the armour mentioned by Alan Lowen melts, men and women, tired of the conflict created by mutual attack and defence games, are becoming friends and companions – equals – seeking intimacy rather than hostility. Role-swapping, in the sense of women going to work and men staying at home to look after the children, is now quite common, whereas a few years ago it was considered peculiar. It is a move towards becoming more conscious, loving human beings instead of aggressively male or female.

Overcoming the negative

In spite of this we still have a long way to go. The increase of absent fathers, indifferent mothers, the consequences of growing up in a culture riddled with guilt and anger, and in families where power is called love (I love you if you do what I want) continue to affect us all as we move into the next century. An angry or unhappy woman can so easily become the witch-mother or hag, whose negative energy paralyses her children and stifles their creativity. Lots of women resent being women, resent being mothers (often especially of daughters) and survive on will-power and attempts to act the perfect mother.

This kind of negative, devouring, 'nothing can please' female energy has left many men afraid of the power of women, and can lead to passive aggression (doing things to wound, without saying a word) and even violence. Lots of young men today are too passive and live at home well into their 30s and 40s, often supported by ageing parents, without making any attempt to create a life of their own. Women without husbands sometimes end up treating their sons as substitute husbands/companions and make it very difficult for them to leave home. If a son does get away in this situation he often suffers inordinate guilt, usually from the mother demanding to know where he is, what he is doing, and 'how can you leave me alone like this?'

A father who is too powerful can push, drive, control, judge and criticise to the point where he too annihilates his children, until they become either perfectionistic hard workers, or irresponsible beach bums. Daughters with this type of father will try too hard to please men, while at the same time not trusting them. Absent fathers cause a similar result.

In some of my workshops I use Mandala drawing as a key to self-assessment. Women who consciously or unconsciously express the 'witch-mother' syndrome, together with the men or women who had or have 'witch-mothers', tend to use excessive dark holly or ivy green in their drawings. One woman, amazed at the truth of what her drawings revealed, went home and questioned her three teenage children about what they thought and felt about her as a mother. She was shocked to discover that they were all afraid of her and felt unable to live up to (what were to them) her unreasonable demands and expectations. She realised that she had spent years trying to be the 'perfect mother', mainly out of guilt because she secretly felt unhappy and unfulfilled in the role. Her attitude to her children came out of the unrealistic demands she put on herself. Although her realisation was extremely painful, she was eventually able to let go of the 'ideal image' she had spent years projecting on her family and friends, and was subsequently much happier.

Women who seek approval and attention from men, or who need to placate them, tend to use a lot of orange, whereas men who use orange in drawing make a statement of a healthy acceptance of their masculinity. Women who use blue show the same acceptance of their femininity, while men who use too much blue are often passive and/or overwhelmed by the idea of female energy. Men and women dominated by both parents frequently use a predominance of deep purple/violet.

In a wonderful film series about men and women Robert Bly (author of *Iron John*) and Marion Woodman (a Jungian analyst and author of many books) tell and interpret an ancient fairy-tale where many of these issues are discussed. They show us how, despite dark moments of despair and loneliness, we can all build creative and empowering relationships. In the process we must find and remove the obstacles which prevent us from fulfilling our innermost longings. When this is done it leads to the marriage or merging of our inner masculine and feminine powers, and so to a dynamic transformation of our outer relationships. These films suggest that although the world is wounded and we ourselves are wounded, when we meet at the point of our woundedness a great healing can take place. (For information on where to obtain these films, please see the back of this book.)

Giving up one's baggage

During my travels I worked, met and lived with hundreds of people who had broken some invisible barrier and crossed a frontier into a country where everything was possible. To do this the old identity had to be dropped, as if the passports to cross this frontier were no longer valid. Ironically this truth was about to be driven home to me only too uncomfortably.

In fact no sooner had I had this thought about passports suddenly losing their potency than I found myself travelling in Europe, giving seminars on meditation, dreams, journal-writing, stress release, crystals and healing.

One day, on a train between Holland and Germany, the police asked for my passport and, having seen it, said they wanted further proof of my identity. As I planned only one night in Germany to see friends before travelling to America to attend a cancer conference, I was travelling light. So light I only had a handbag and toothbrush with me – even my plane tickets were in Amsterdam.

Refusing to accept this the police took me off the train and put me in a cell in the local police station, from where they said they would call the foreign office in London. I opened my bag to read an article by Jerry Jampolski, whom I was to introduce at the cancer conference, and found the headlines: 'Have you ever felt lonely, unloved and depressed? Have you ever felt locked up, pushed in a corner where you cannot get out?' I closed my eyes and said, 'God, why is this happening to me?' When I opened my eyes a few minutes later I saw on a bench in the opposite corner the book *I Never Promised You a Rose Garden*. It seemed a pretty direct answer to my question.

Three days later, with the help of the local British consul, and having missed my original plane, I arrived in New York. Ecstatic to be out of the police cell and standing on the free, welcoming shores of America, I presented my passport to the control. Two seconds later a heavy hand fell on my shoulder and, categorised as an undesirable alien, I was marched off for what turned out to be a long and intense interrogation.

'Who are you? What do you do?' I was asked by a burly, uniformed man. Thinking that stress-release sounded less airy-fairy than meditation I replied, 'I teach stress-release'. He gazed at me while opening my suitcase, strewing its contents over the counter between us. My appointment diary lay on the top of the pile and picking it up he read a poem I'd copied out of a recipe book which began, 'I want to live to be an outrageous old woman and not an old lady. I want to have ten thousand lovers in one love.'

He missed the first two lines, as well as the words 'in one love', and ran a finger along to 'I want to have ten thousand lovers.' Incredulous he said, 'You call this stress-release? We have another name for it here.'

I was doomed. I had money of different denominations from the workshops I'd given in different European countries which was going to a community in America, together with notes, most of them still unread, saying things like 'My few hours with you have changed my life.' No matter how hard I tried to prove myself – showing the invitations to lecture, the temporary visa that indicated I was not planning to stay – nor what I said, he would not move an inch from the idea of the ten thousand lovers and what that implied to him.

Suddenly a gun went off. I leaped back and looked round to see a man in Arab clothes lying on the floor in a pool of blood.

Sick with shock, as if the strings holding my bones together had been cut, I watched the room fill with uniformed men. Doctors, nurses, ambulance men and a stretcher appeared. After what seemed an eternity and much discussion, the man was removed.

'Why did you do that?' I asked.

'It was him or us,' was the reply. 'Besides, we only shoot to wound, not to kill.'

They turned their attention back to me. 'Now who are you, really?' To explain their ferocity, months later I discovered that the German police had alerted New York because they suspected I was part of the Baader-Meinhof Gang.

Having spent five hours – and three days before this – trying to prove who I was, I suddenly felt it was irrelevant and did not matter.

'I am,' I answered.

'You're what?'

'I am.'

'What does that mean, I am?'

'I just am. I have nothing else to say.'

He shrugged, repacked my suitcase, handed it to me and let me go. I realised that as soon as I dropped all desire to prove or explain myself, let go of who I thought I was or ought to be, life moved on again.

Movements of awareness

Across the globe hundreds of others were also discovering and expressing new, true identities. In England, the Findhorn Foundation, the Wrekin Trust founded by Sir George Trevelyan, and the Festival for Mind, Body and Spirit started by Graham Wilson in 1977, introduced people to ideas that seemed so way out that the press deemed the festival a collection of cranks.

Graham conceived the idea after trying to find for himself answers to questions about religion, philosophy, astrology and numerous other subjects. He realised other people probably had similar questions and so, hiring Olympia – normally used for shows such as the Ideal Home Exhibition – he gathered together a vast array of people and information. In order to pay for this Graham mortgaged his house, so strong was his belief in his idea of the Festival.

Olympia was filled with the sounds of hundreds of people experimenting with yoga, dowsing, aura reading, telepathy, UFO discoveries, teaching the blind to see through developing inner or psychic senses, dance, vegetarianism, clairvoyance, T'ai Chi, reincarnation, philosophy, religion, mind-control, spiritual healing, meditation, and psychic sciences such as palm and tarot reading, to name but a few. They learned about crystals, kinesiology, wholefood, planetary chakras, Kirlian photography, ley lines, herbal remedies, massage, water-births, aromatherapy, standing stones, pyramidology and the secret life of plants.

At one festival there was a greenhouse which monitored the plants' reaction to people passing by. At another, hundreds danced around a maypole before having their hands, heads or hearts read through psychic readings, which often included a drawing of their spirit guide. Some came to buy a stick of incense and found new meaning and purpose to life. Others came out of curiosity or to meet a friend. All discovered a thousand and one different routes to self-fulfilment and understanding, from baking organic bread to healing a faltering relationship. Even the cloakroom attendants commented on the atmosphere in which not one child cried or got lost and people were happy and smiling.

Newspaper reporters who had initially poured scorn on the festival came back to find mile-long queues of people waiting to get in, and started to write, 'Maybe 100,000 people can't be wrong. Something is going on.'

The Wrekin Trust and the Festival for Mind, Body and Spirit made available to the general public people like Paul Solomon, sometimes called the modern Edgar Cayce; Hans Selye, a specialist in stress and ageing problems; Norman Cousins, former editor of the *New Yorker* who wrote the book *Anatomy of an Illness* after healing a supposedly incurable disease with carefully prescribed doses of laughter; Admiral Shattock who, despite advice to have surgery, healed an arthritic hip with mind power and visualisation. Indian gurus such as Muktenanda and

Rajneesh were extremely popular and Sai Baba, whose teaching is based on the oneness between God and creation, drew hundreds of followers to his ashram in India to see for themselves the sacred ash (or Vibhuti) and jewels he produced out of the air. Numerous healers such as Rose Gladden, Andrew Watson and many, many more demonstrated the transference of mental and physical energy in healing.

Close Encounters of the Third Kind and the *Star Wars* series, later followed by *ET*, opened people's minds to the possibility of UFOs and extra-terrestrial communication. I remember going to the press showing of *Close Encounters* before it hit the general cinema route and the whole audience of 'seen-it-all-before' entertainment critics rose to their feet and clapped. Films on reincarnation such as *Heaven Can Wait*, followed later by *Field of Dreams, Dead Again, Truly, Madly, Deeply, Ghost* and *Always* – together with television and news articles on near-death experiences – reflected the changing awareness and interests sweeping through people's minds.

As impressive an opening to this new awareness was Findhorn, mentioned in the previous chapter. Starting off as an apparent giant vegetable-growing experiment, it has become a community of people devoted to personal development and healing the planet. Initially based on Eileen's guidance from God, it gradually expanded to each person learning to trust their own guidance, and take responsibility for themselves and the community. Whether a person came for two weeks or five years their lives were profoundly changed. Many have taken what they learned back into their own countries and communities and inspired others as Peter and Eileen Caddy inspired them.

I went to Findhorn expecting magic and was put to work on maintenance – cleaning out blocked loos or scrubbing bricks – and otherwise cooking in the kitchen. I learned that work was love in action and that total acceptance by others of who we are, in the moment, can catalyse complete change. I found that every nook and cranny of garden, hotel (the community finally took over the Cluny hotel from which Peter had been fired), community buildings and caravans reflected the love and attention put into them. The flowers seemed more colourful, the people taller, brighter and shinier than outside the community and even the machinery – whether for garden, house or kitchen – operated cheerfully in response to being thanked. Everyone and everything was treated with respect and care.

Despite, or maybe because of, cleaning blocked loos and scrubbing bricks, I had some extraordinary spiritual experiences. Whether meditating in the Sanctuary or simply sitting outside on the grass, I frequently felt hands rest on my shoulders and then had a sense of liquid gold being poured into my body through the top of my head to the tips of my toes. I felt every cell in my body tingle and glow. For days afterwards whatever I touched sparked as if a match had been struck.

I climbed mountains in Bulgaria and discovered a brotherhood, with whom I am still involved, who showed me the meaning of truth, purity and simplicity in spiritual development. Their work, based on the teachings of Beinsa Douna, sometimes known as Peter Deunov, encourages the same principles as Findhorn of love, work and spiritual discipline. Beinsa Douna's work, which emphasised love of God and union with God, had its source in the Orphic mysteries of Thrace (now Bulgaria) which flowed through Pythagoras and Plato into esoteric Christianity, through the Essenes and Christian Gnostics, through the Bogomils and Cathars – both of which movements called themselves the friends of God. He had at least 40,000 followers before the war and, as a result of the greater freedom in the East since the collapse of Communism, his teaching is now re-emerging.

For me to camp and climb in Bulgaria, waking at 4am to greet the rising sun, dancing the series of meditational movements of paneurhythmy, set to music and words composed by Beinsa Douna himself, to be surrounded by the extraordinary atmosphere of the Rila mountains and the sense of the presence of this great teacher, was like a living meditation. I had experiences of shrinking to a grain of sand and expanding to include the whole universe. I had visions of great spiritual presence, beings of light pouring energy into the Earth which I saw as a violet ray of transformation, bringing changes which were not always comfortable. Each visit transformed and healed me.

Time seemed to be speeding up, both horizontal and vertical

time – inner and outer – as if civilisation had started on the outside edge of a long-playing gramophone record and, like a gramophone needle speeds up as it moves from the wider circumference to the narrower bit near the hole in the middle, was now spinning faster. We are finishing a phase of evolution and getting ready to plop through the 'hole in the middle' and start the next phase.

Entering the void

Individually many people have gone into this hole which can give a sense of void or being in limbo. The void can be black, like the dark night of the soul, which rips away the fabric and foundation of our lives, moves us from breakdown to breakthrough. The phrase 'dark night of the soul' comes from writings of the Spanish mystic, St John of the Cross. Today it implies the crisis when the things that used to work for us no longer do. If we find ourselves in a dark void we need to remember that a seed grows buried in dark soil. It needs the dark to germinate and bring forth new life.

We can be catapulted into a dark night of the soul after success as much as after failure. Instead of the expected elation of having achieved what we may have spent years striving for, we suddenly feel flat, empty and depressed. This happened to me after I completed my first book, *The Power of Gems and Crystals*. Instead of relief and excitement, a part of me said: 'So what? I'll probably never have another idea and will never write another book.'

Lao Tzu, the Chinese sage, described the void as 'the nothingness out of which everything came'. In other words it is the source of all creation, the sea of limitless potential.

Today many people are frightened by the thought of emptiness or an empty space and try to fill it with frenetic activity. If instead we could welcome what is literally a breathing space between one phase of life and another, relinquish the past, surrender ourselves to the void (whether black or white), and merge with it, we will discover exactly what we must do next.

For eons of time masculine or yang energy – analytic, intellectual, thrusting, aggressive, powerful and outwardly active – has dominated the Earth and all life upon it. As we move into the next millennium we increasingly recognise and relate to the power of the feminine, Gaia, goddess or yin energy, which is receptive, intuitive, imaginative; which listens, feels and nurtures from the heart rather than from the head.

The more outwardly active we are, the more likely it is that life will push us into what appears to be an empty space in order to be still, to listen, to feel and learn from within rather than following directions from without. In the process we also assimilate the new energies that pour into the planet from all sides instead of letting them wash over us like water off a duck's back.

We can also experience a white void in which there is a sense of excitement that something is about to happen, even if we are not sure yet what it will be; it is like coming to a crossroads where there is no sign and we wait to see what to do next.

Some of us suddenly realise that we stand at the crossroads alone. As we look around for the friends or companions who were there one minute and gone the next, there is a temptation to turn back. When Lot's wife turned back she was crystallised into a pillar of salt. No matter how lonely or confused we may feel, we must keep our eyes, ears, hearts and minds open for what lies ahead. Instead of waiting for others to empower us we must empower ourselves.

From a point of total lack of self-worth and powerlessness, I used to pray for the power to serve God and the world. It seemed as if my prayers would never be answered, so one day I went outside and, with my bare feet on the earth, yelled to the sky, 'Hey God – I have a right to the power of my own being and my own experience. I want it now – I claim it *now*.' I suddenly felt a whoosh of energy surge through me until every cell in my body tingled. I realised that most of us run around feeling helpless and powerless when all we have to do is ask for power and open ourselves to it.

The power I refer to is not that of an authority figure but the power that comes when we acknowledge our connection to the source of life – to limitless love and infinite wisdom. This power can be used to change every aspect of life and means that no matter what happens around us we can become spiritually fearless.

Personal power is a joyous energy which is part of our birthright. If you do not wish to claim it as I did, *visualise* asking for it and imagine the light or colour of power pouring in through the top of your head until your whole body is radiating its energy. Or visualise a symbol of power or a power animal whose qualities you draw on when you need them. It can also help to imagine a symbol for your masculine power in your right hand and another symbol for your feminine power in your left hand. Spend time imagining the weight, colour, size and qualities of each and then merge them together and bring them into your heart. You could also draw or make a collage of images that sum up your own ideas of personal power and place it where you see it every day. You could ask for a dream to help you or invite the Angel of Power into your life. No matter what method you use, remember to express the energy and to use it with joy.

Humanity is undergoing a major initiation. Initiation simply means a change, a move from one level of perception to another. Throughout life we experience both minor and major initiations. A minor initiation tends to feel major because it usually involves strong emotion. For example, my fiancé runs off with another woman, or I lose my job. However, I continue to live in the same house and area, see the same friends and, apart from the pain, life continues as before. By contrast, a major initiation is life-changing and it sometimes takes months to realise that our present taste in clothes, friends, food and life-style is so completely different from the past that it is almost like another incarnation.

The biggest mistake we can make at this time is to do nothing. Many of us recognise this but are so afraid of making a mistake, we sit glued to our seats waiting for the hand of God to drop out of the sky with a sign to make everything clear. We must use this time to explore our inner selves through meditation, visualisation and dreams; purify our physical bodies, examine how our thoughts and emotions create our reality and change them if life is not good. Above all, we should do as much as we can to celebrate life with joy, laughter, love and delight. The time of growth through pain and suffering is over – the time of growth through happiness is here.

Opening ourselves up to change

The consciousness of the planet is lifting to another level as if the chakras of the Earth were opening and expanding. Chakra in Sanskrit means 'wheel' and each chakra in the human body is a whirring vortex of energy, vibrating at different frequencies. The lowest three chakras vibrate at a lower frequency than do the heart, throat, third eye and crown chakra. As the heart chakra of the Earth expands – which has been happening for the last thirty to forty years, as we move into the fourth dimension and prepare for the fifth – we experience the vibrational frequency of the planet speeding up, a sense of accelerated change.

This change stimulates transformation similar to a Kundalini awakening. Kundalini is a Sanskrit word that means 'coiled serpent'. It refers to the energy coiled in a ball at the base of the spine which, when activated, rises up, igniting and expanding the chakras, until it bursts through the tip of a person's head. It is said that once Kundalini energy rises, enlightenment occurs and reunion with God is possible. To see with enlightened vision means we accept the perfection of, and recognise our oneness with, all that exists. We live from the heart. However, if we are not spiritually and physically prepared, Kundalini energy can lead to breakdown rather than breakthrough. Spiritual teachers suggest that their students must purify mind, body and emotions so that what amounts to a major vibrational shift – like being struck by lightning – can occur without danger to the personality.

If we can move with this acceleration life can be full of excitement; if not we'll experience fear, panic and life in chaos while we adjust to it. It can also produce uncomfortable physical, mental and emotional side effects which I will discuss in the next chapter.

No matter whether these past years have inspired us to change voluntarily, or because life fell apart through loss of job, health or relationship, the Great Mother Earth on which we live is shaking us awake, forcing us to put our lives in order and take note of what is going on around us. In the process we have to clear our emotional bodies which, like soggy sponges, have absorbed everything that has ever happened to us – from this and other lives. Whether it be re-birthing, co-counselling, past-life therapy or any of the myriad other forms of help, the techniques made available to us during the past thirty or forty years are carefully designed to aid us. So are some of the life situations that squeeze our emotional bodies dry, thus enabling us finally to act rather than react, live rather than just survive.

By thinking differently – by acting instead of reacting – we can tap into limitless creativity, infinite possibilities. In fact these years have been pushing us all to stand up and act rather than react.

A few years ago I was in Los Angeles and met a man who knew Emmet Fox, the writer and philosopher, when he first arrived in America. He told me this story about Emmet's first visit to a self-service restaurant.

Never having been in one before, he sat and waited to be served, becoming increasingly impatient at being unable to attract the attention of a waiter or waitress, and even more so when he realised that other people who came in after him were now sitting in front of steaming plates of food.

Finally, thoroughly exasperated, he got up and approached a man at a nearby table and said: 'I've been sitting here for twenty minutes without anyone taking a bit of notice. Now I see that you, who came in five minutes ago, sit here with a complete meal in front of you. What's going on? How do you get served in this country?'

The man, astonished, replied: 'But this is a self-service restaurant!' He pointed to the far end of the room where food was abundantly displayed. 'Go over there, take a tray, choose exactly what you want, pay for it, then sit down and eat it!'

Feeling a little silly, Emmet Fox followed the man's instructions and, as he put the food on the table, it suddenly struck him that life itself was a self-service restaurant. All manner of events, opportunities, situations, joys, delights and sadnesses are set out before us, and most of us remain fixed, bottoms glued to our seats, so busy looking at what everyone else has on their plates, wondering, 'Why has he got jelly and ice-cream? Why has she got a bigger helping?' that it never occurs to us simply to get up, see what is available, and choose what we want. When we do, to quote Sun Bear again, 'We will realise the generous and loving nature that is ours just as it is a part of all creation.'

3

SYMPTOMS
OF CHANGE

In the massive shift which is taking place on every level of
existence, from planetary to sub-atomic, many of us are
experiencing great discomfort. Across the world for the past
thirty years, I saw, and still see, the same symptoms coming up:
chronic, glandular-fever type tiredness in which people feel so
droopy that they can hardly put one foot in front of another; the
sense of time speeding by so fast that there is never enough time
– even children feel this.

To live in the fourth dimension means we have 20 per cent less
time and everything takes 20 per cent more time to do, so it is
essential to focus on priorities. For example, stop dusting or
cleaning the car every day and write the book you always
wanted to write, or read one someone else wrote that can
expand your consciousness.

Psychics and channels tell us that our physical bodies, as well
as every particle of life on earth, are being accelerated in energy,
vibration and consciousness to the maximum that we can
withstand in every 24-hour period. Not only does this cause
physical discomfort, but it also pushes to the surface old
behaviour-patterns and irrational fears (which I discuss
throughout the book) and makes things appear as if they are
getting worse. Most of the anxiety, panic and desperation comes

from our egos who, fearing annihilation and loss of control, try to manipulate and intimidate us.

According to Patti Diane Cota-Robles, founder of the New Age Study of Humanity's Purpose in Tucson, Arizona, we are going through an unprecedented crash course to prepare us for our solar passage into the fifth dimension. She says that this is a unique experiment – 'Never in the history of the universe has the planet been given the opportunity to pass through two-dimensional shifts in such a short period of time.'

For a long time I myself have thought that we skimmed through the fourth dimension, rather like a pebble skimming the surface of a pond, and have been in a space where the fourth and fifth dimensions interface. When this occurs, time, space, spirit and matter merge, and we experience No Time. Ancient calendars such as the Chinese, Tibetan, Egyptian and Mayan not only end now, but point to this time as being unique and important, which adds to our sense of No Time. Things appear and disappear. Incidents of synchronicity and forgetfulness increase. Many of us experience these symptoms, but most books focus on the move from the third to the fourth dimensions, rather than from the fourth to the fifth. So I was relieved to discover that Patti was of a like mind.

The Hopi Indians also speak of humanity's life in other worlds, and say we are now in the fifth, which will heal the separation between man's head and heart.

Across the world thousands of people anxiously await the arrival of the Photon Belt, which is a band of light discovered by satellite in 1961. A photon is a quantum (smallest particle) of electromagnetic energy with zero mass – i.e. no electrical charge and indefinite lifetime. Deepak Chopra said the following about the Photon Belt:

Before the sun throws out light, where is the light? Photons come out of nowhere, they cannot be stored, can barely be pinned down in time, and have no home in space whatsoever. That is, light occupies no volume and no mass. The similarity between a photon and a thought is very deep. Both are born in a region beyond space and time, where nature controls all processes in that void which is full of creative intelligence.

While some wait for the light of the Photon Belt to penetrate the Earth, others believe it already has, and that when we reach its midpoint, cataclysmic changes will take place. This light will supposedly trigger the release of all negative karma and enable humanity to drop pre-conceived egocentric ideas, to gain release from the physical body, and to become astral-travelling, multi-dimensional beings. Meanwhile we must love and care for one another, the Earth and everything in it, including ourselves, as best we can.

If any of these ideas cause anxiety, you may like to try the following exercise, which I use myself when I have to become calm and centred. I close my eyes and take two or three deep breaths in through my nose and out through my mouth. I then imagine a light above the top of my head, and breathe it into my heart. At the same time I slowly affirm: 'I am ... I am ... I am ... I am one with the Source of all life. I am one with the Heart, the Body, the Mind of God. I am loved. I am love.' On each slow in-breath I bring the light deeper into my heart, and on each slow out-breath I expand the light into every cell, tissue and organ. This can be used for one minute or ten or twenty. I always feel immediate strength and peace.

Relationships

This loss of time experienced in the fourth dimension can also induce a feeling of losing control of one's life. 'Not only are my relationships falling apart but I can no longer keep my cupboards and drawers tidy. Everything is in chaos from kitchen to office desk.' Relationships are increasingly difficult to sustain because we have got to become whole and secure within ourselves without being totally dependent on someone else.

The average marriage or relationship starts off with a scenario something like this. I, Jane, not feeling too sure of myself, am delighted to be invited out. I put on my best clothes and best behaviour. Because I am insecure, a few outings down the line I am unconsciously going to show my date/admirer how awful I believe I am. I throw a tantrum. He either recoils and disappears from my life or shrugs, thinks I am in a strange mood but our apparent previous compatibility merits hanging in there. I am initially relieved but then – again unconsciously – think, 'If I'm so awful and he thinks I'm OK he can't be so hot himself.'

I begin in various ways, big and small, to treat him with contempt. He in turn does the same to me. I also show him what buttons he can press in me by my reactions to what he does and says. If we do not feel secure in ourselves we end up in unhealthy situations of button-pushing – which gives us a false sense of power – while propping each other up in-between.

Instead of looking outside for what we need from someone else, we must look within. The collapse of even loving, supportive relationships now push many men and women to do just that. If we stop projecting on to the people around us our own imbalance – or lack of empathy with our own inner male and female – which usually comes from poor relationships with our parents, life can change dramatically.

Marriage or commitment to another person takes courage. We tend to forget that we not only take on the bits we know and like in the other person but also the unknown, the nasty or difficult, the Jungian shadow. Most relationships fail when we enter them for the wrong reasons – such as fear, loneliness, sex, boredom, recovery from problems or previous rejection. We want more out of them than we wish to put in.

Paul Solomon once said he could tell a person's relationship with life itself by observing his/her attitude to a Coke machine. People come along, shove their money in a slot – neither too much nor too little – and impatiently wait for their demand to be met. He said that nine out of ten people kick or shake the machine in a vain attempt to make it deliver what they want more quickly. We demand and expect the same response from our spouses and lovers and woe betide them if our needs are not instantly met.

It is impossible for one man or one woman to fulfil all needs or to express every aspect of masculine and feminine energy. The purpose of a relationship is not to capture or hold another, nor to find someone who makes us feel whole but to share our wholeness in order to see who we really are.

A relationship is a journey in self-discovery and must begin with self-love and self-acceptance. If I honour myself and my feelings, I will honour my partner and give both of us the space to grow and to be. For a partnership to succeed we all need to be self-conscious, self-aware and even selfish. To constantly put another person's needs before our own (I do not refer to the requirements or demands made on us by illness or disability) can finally lead to resentment. Loss of self and identity cause more pain and problems than anything else.

Relationships do not simply consist of men and women living, loving and bouncing off each other but reflect our attitude to God, work, money, houses, gardens, animals, ideas, objects, nature and machinery. We relate to all things, whether concrete or abstract.

In the past we entered temples, monasteries and mystery schools to know God and discover the truth about ourselves. Today life itself is the mystery school and a relationship is the temple through which we learn the curriculum. As Rilke wrote: 'To love is good too – love being difficult. For one human being to love another: that is perhaps the most difficult of all our tasks, the ultimate, the last test and proof; the work for which all other work is but a preparation.'

Sexuality

Men and women are becoming androgynous – a combination of male and female, with neither predominant. As a result our views of sex are also changing. These views are conditioned by the society in which we live. The Victorians were so prudish and overtly fearful of seduction that they not only wore three or four layers of clothing in bed but also covered the legs of the tables from which they ate. In contrast Rome, under Caligula, showed the most arrant licentiousness and sexual cruelty. In Greece the practice by the elite – especially in Plato's time – of homosexuality, combined with the social duty of marriage, was completely normal. Currently, ideal sex should include body, mind, spirit and feeling. The problems we may now have about sex are not about sex itself but how we think about sex.

If you or I grew up in a family where it was totally acceptable to run around naked or to see our parents naked, we are likely to be far more comfortable with our own bodies and therefore our sexuality. The way in which we first learn about sex can also affect our attitude to it. When she was seven years old one of my patients was told by her mother, in response to a question about sex (having overheard the word in the school toilet), 'Never go near a Chinese man, they breed like rabbits.' This was the sum total of her sex education. A few months later, going to see a friend who lived in a block of flats, she found herself in a lift with a Chinese man. She shrank away from him but for two or three years afterwards was both terrified, and convinced that she was pregnant. She had absolutely no knowledge of what happened to cause pregnancy.

A friend, sent to a Catholic boarding school, was indoctrinated with the idea that even to see another girl naked was a mortal sin. These were eight- and nine-year-old children. Another friend, male, given the same message by the brothers at his school, became traumatised by the memory of seeing the three-year-old sister of a friend naked in her bath. This, he was told, damned him to eternal hellfire. He was about ten years old at the time. This kind of indoctrination can (although not always of course) lead to sexual impotence or 'furtive sex' in the sense of secret titillation from nudity, whether on the beach or through pornographic magazines and clubs.

Human sexuality is based on the desire to commune with or be at one with another person (you and I are one). It is a communication underneath which is the desire to be at one with God. In fact when there is a problem with communication in a marriage there is usually a problem with sex and vice versa. Whether we love each other, animals, our environment or crystals and stones, it is all part of the same instinctive desire for oneness. Therefore, however love comes, we need to celebrate it.

Sexuality leads us towards enlightenment. Passion is part of compassion: you cannot have one without the other. I read recently that sexual energy is 'close' to spiritual energy. I do not believe there is a difference. There is the undifferentiated energy of the universe which we use for running, talking, walking, baking a cake or making love. It is the energy of creation. We should not repress it but instead decide, or be aware of, how we channel it.

In Ruth White's book *Sexuality and Spirituality*, Gildas, Ruth's discarnate teacher and guide, says:

> Sex is indeed a deep mystery. At its highest level and with all that it can awaken, it holds in a sense the keys to the purpose of existence. It connects with creation, with the earth energies and with all the elements. It is a force of high communion between male and female and as such can lead to a sense of completion and the experience of God-likeness. . . . Communion through sexuality can lead to the awareness of the angels, the source, the divine and the principle of co-creatorship.

In the past, priests and priestesses were taught how to channel this energy, or life-force, for clairvoyance, telepathy and healing as well as for sacred rituals within the temples. In fact during one of Paul Solomon's early readings for a cancer patient, he was told that the stimulation of sexual energy could lead to a cure. This was done by the patient's wife, giving her husband a twice-daily massage around the lower abdomen and groin. The man recovered – not as the result of sexual activity, but because his life-force was stimulated in such a way he could direct it to the cancerous cells.

Many Eastern religions – especially Indian – depict statues and pictures of male and female genitalia, as well as dozens of different sexual positions on temple walls. Sex was sacred and every act of sexual union was a way to reach spiritual fulfilment.

Unfortunately in the West, many religions teach us that sex is either sinful or solely for procreation. We grow up with no understanding of the connection between sexuality, spirituality and creativity.

The 1990s' acceptance of sperm-bank parenthood, surrogate

mothers, artificial insemination, in-vitro fertilisation, genetic manipulation and cloning, separate the sexual act from tenderness, touch, intimacy and spiritual fulfilment. Hormone treatments that allows sixty-year-old women to conceive, vasectomy, the Pill and abortion have all contributed to the dehumanisation of life, both sexually and spiritually.

A psychiatrist, Karl Munchen, told me that the majority of his teenage patients who attempt, or successfully commit, suicide do so as a result of the disappointment of their first sexual encounter. Most advertising revolves around sex in one form or another. If we smoke, eat, drink, read, drive or wear what is upmarket and fashionable, we are assured of sexual success. Karl says that this kind of advertising leads children to believe that all problems will be solved and life will bloom as soon as they find a sexual partner. Some of his patients are only nine or ten years old.

We need to remember that sex is an expression of love and joy and can enable us to attune to nature, colour, art and music as well as a heightened sense of all that is spiritual and sacred. Instead of reducing the sexual experience to a means of increasing sales of instant coffee, we should celebrate what ought to be one of the most powerful, exciting, renewing, invigorating and intimate of human and spiritual experiences available to us on this planet.

Homosexuality, confusion and guilt

Human love is not a substitute for spiritual love but an aspect of it. In this sense homosexuality is as relevant as any other kind of loving. It is based on the same instinctive desire for oneness. A few years ago much of my work involved homosexuality. This included both men and women who had sex change operations.

Homosexuality combines confusion – 'I feel female in a male body' or vice versa – with the need to reinforce male or female energy, which may have been missing since childhood, as well as a refusal to deal with the spiritual lessons chosen for this life. In every case there was a pattern of guilt and lack of self-acceptance.

John Bradshaw, a counsellor who specialises in family therapy, describes this pattern as a 'toxic shame'. 'Toxic shame' is the feeling of being flawed and defective as a human person, whether male or female.

Guilt says: 'I *made* a mistake.' 'Toxic shame' says: 'I *am* a mistake.'

This shame affects, to some degree or another, 98 per cent of humanity and is a major contributing cause of our massive addiction problems as well as unhealthy relationships with each other. It is imperative to recognise and heal this wound, much of which comes from family training that encourages us to repress emotion and not say how we really feel.

To change sex on the outside will not automatically change how we feel on the inside. One of my sex-change clients, now a woman having previously been a husband, and father of an eleven-year-old daughter, was still desperately unhappy and insecure three years after the operation. In the middle of a particularly traumatic and difficult session I suddenly heard the sound of laughter fill the room.

I looked up and had a vision of a group of hierarchical beings standing around helpless with mirth at how seriously, and guiltily, we deal with our sexuality. I saw an image of humanity as two- and three-year-old children playing in a sandpit with no clothes on and exploring their differences – which, after all, we have been given to explore. I realised that our teachers and guides look on our antics in the same way we would our own two- and three-year-old children. Also that the only 'sin' – the word in Greek means 'to miss the mark' – is to deliberately hurt or harm another.

Sharing this vision with my client had a far more profound effect than any 'proper' therapy. She is now getting on with the rest of her life having dropped the baggage of her past.

Confusion about our sexual identity can often be the result of a previous incarnation. I may have, as a woman, fallen madly and passionately in love with a man who in this life has incarnated into a female body. I am now again in a female body and, when we meet, the mutual attraction of the previous life is so strong we enter into a lesbian relationship (or vice-versa – we are now men and enter a homosexual relationship). If I have had a predominance of male or female lives, but am now incarnate in the body of the opposite sex, it might also lead to confusion re my sexual identity.

To develop spiritual understanding requires many lifetimes. These lives present us with every facet of human event and emotion, including homosexuality, which is often chosen by the soul for the experience it brings. We may also choose to be bisexual or homosexual for karmic reasons. The more judgemental we are today about other peoples' sexual preference the more likely we are to be confronted with our prejudice. For example a friend of mine who constantly criticised gay men and women came home one day to find her husband in bed with the milkman and two days later her daughter confessed her lesbian relationships.

These experiences are neither good nor bad (unless we deliberately try to cause hurt) but simply part of our soul search for balance.

Releasing relationships with love

Relationships, whether with men or women, speed our growth. We are attracted to the person or people who will create change within us. Like a mirror image they reflect parts of us we may not recognise without them. This means we come together, not necessarily to stay together, but to grow.

When we have learned what we needed to learn, maybe it is time to move on. If we could have an attitude of 'we will use this relationship to serve our mutual need to be whole', and release it with love when it no longer serves that purpose, the ending of relationships – whether with job, family, lover, house or country – would be far less painful. I do not mean we should abandon our commitments without any attempt to sort out problems. However, we live in a world vastly different from that of our grandparents.

In the current climate of change it may not be possible, or even beneficial for our soul's growth, to stay with one person for sixty or seventy years. Perhaps families of the future will consist of small groups of like-minded people who together contract to bring up children with an option to move on when their task is finished. This might well provide more emotional intimacy than much of our so-called family life today.

We have chosen this life

No matter what happens in the future, we must understand that the purpose of life is spiritual growth. That no thing – person, situation, accident or illness – comes into our lives by mistake. Everything has been carefully chosen; everything that we have set in motion we will meet again, not as punishment but in order to understand the laws of cause and effect. We wrote a script which we then produced, directed and acted in. We chose our parents as well as many of the problems we now complain about.

In fact the people who have been the most difficult and unlovable are probably the ones who love us the most. For example, before coming to Earth I may recognise that I had a previous life as a tyrant and bully. I now decide to experience what it feels like to be on the receiving end of this treatment. I run around saying to members of my soul family, or other friends: 'I have to go to Earth again and live out another life. Please would one of you play the part of a bullying, arrogant father?'

Most of them say: 'No – we have other things to do.' Again and again I ask. Finally someone says: 'Well, I do not want to do it, but because I love you and know it will help you to evolve and grow, I will.' This entity descends into the Earth plane. I later become his daughter and, when he bullies me, bemoan my fate. 'Why me? Why do I have to suffer like this?', completely forgetting that I created the situation in the first place.

Most of us forget that we have the power to choose our response to everything that happens in our lives. Our souls lead us to the exact opportunities we need to experience in this life – the actual experience depends on how we respond to the opportunity.

Conception, birth and self-worth

Not only do we choose our parents but we also participate in the moment of our conception. Our consciousness enters the auric field of the mother six weeks before she conceives. The attitude of the man and woman (who ultimately become our parents) to each other, both sexually and emotionally, in that moment affect our acceptance or rejection of our own male and female qualities.

We identify with it, good, bad or indifferent – which affects our self-worth as well as our ability to enjoy sex. The attitude of the woman at the moment of knowing she is pregnant – not by intuition or imagination, but by the physical fact of the doctor telling her this is so – also affects our self-acceptance and identity. If I, as the mother, am either unmarried, unprepared or pregnant for the nineteenth time, I might say, 'Oh, *no*! It's too soon, too late or too much.' If the personality coming in identifies with this reaction – in other words, 'I am the cause of fear, unhappiness and resistance' – it will inevitably feel guilty and unworthy.

Another cause of guilt and inadequacy comes from our discarnate reaction to being told we must come to Earth again. Much of my individual work goes into this area, as I find many people's reaction to the thought of leaving the inbetween-life planes, which are ones of peace, learning and love, is frequently one of shock, fear, pain and resistance. This resistance can cause us to hold back on life and be fearful of freely expressing ourselves. In addition we may choose, from a soul perspective, a body that is physically inadequate, a mind that is limited in intelligence, and an emotional sensitivity that makes us extremely vulnerable. When we are at one with the soul in these other dimensions, our choices appear full of excitement. As we descend through the planes, pre-conception, we put on the limitations in consciousness of these different bodies that we have chosen and it can sometimes feel too much. It is similar to putting on a scuba-diving outfit. Until we get into the water, the suit feels unbearably heavy and the wetsuit, goggles and flippers too tight and restrictive. In other words, some of our lack of self-worth is set in motion long before birth.

Future generations must learn the spiritual significance of pre-conception, conception, birth and early childhood. Meanwhile, if we gave more attention to babies and children when they are laughing and happy, and less when they scream and behave badly, we would begin to sow seeds of – 'I matter more when I am happy than when I am sad.' This in turn would help change our unconscious adult patterns of sometimes becoming sick to draw attention to ourselves when we feel unloved and depressed.

In my book *Journeys Through Time* I describe various regression techniques that can be used for both the past of this present life and the past of other lives. They include a journey back into the moment of conception, to the attitude of the parents to each other at conception, the nine months of pregnancy and the moment of birth. The key to the success of any of these inner journeys is total relaxation – physical, mental and emotional – which can be done through exercise, deep breathing and visualising a happy or special place. Another journey in which we can discover our attitude to coming to Earth is to imagine moving upwards as if a balloon or bubble were gently lifting out of the top of our heads and drifting through time and space until it arrives in a space between lives. Visualise a teacher or guide saying 'It is time to leave this place – time to go – time to go to Earth', and re-experience your reaction (sometimes this works better with someone else's voice to guide).

We can also visualise our mental, emotional and physical spiritual bodies and ask why we chose them, what lessons we were meant to learn through them, have we done so, what do they need now, how can we heal them, etc. Finally, blend them together and fill them with light.

Change and dis-ease

Depression, apprehension, vague feelings of dis-ease, as well as any confusion arising from the break-up of family life and relationships as we have known them, are also common symptoms of the changes we are moving through.

Our immune system is breaking down and we are suffering, like the Earth, from an overdose of toxicity. Cancer, together with Aids and TB – now becoming as much of a problem as Aids – are symbolic of the Earth's problems. Cancer is basically a 'selfish' disease. One cell eats another and then another and so on until it finally kills the host on which it lives. Is it not similar to what mankind is doing to the Earth?

Aids, among other things, produces lesions in the skin. The Earth has lesions caused by industrial pollution, nuclear poisoning, acid rain, ozone layer depletion and deforestation – which causes non-arable land and desert.

TB is a disease of the lungs. The trees are the lungs of the Earth and what do we do but cut them down without adequate replacement? Some cultures, such as the Japanese, use the equivalent of a forest a day in disposable chopsticks. We also fill the atmosphere with carbon dioxide from the cars we drive so neither we nor the trees can breathe properly. The collapse of our immune system can also be seen in the increasing number of people – again worldwide – suffering from chronic bronchitis, pneumonia, sinusitis, allergies, coughs, colds and 'flu that will not go away. Others have cramplike pains in the bones and joints, continual sore throats, teeth, mouth and neck problems.

Today, stress and toxic pollutants in the atmosphere are the major cause of degenerative disease. Acid rain, carbon monoxide from cars and cigarettes, insecticides, tap-water laced with chemicals, aluminium, carcinogenic plastics like PVC, radiation from computers, word processors and copy machines affect our immune system. Microwave ovens, TVs, radios, burglar alarms, cellular phones, X-rays, fluorescent lighting, many detergents and household cleaners make us more susceptible to illness. Asthma and pneumonia are increasing to epidemic proportions. In Japan it has been found that children who spend too much time with computers suffer blood cell degeneration.

Poor nourishment creates digestive problems while alcoholism leads to liver, heart and mental disorders. Noise affects our hearing, drugs such as penicillin no longer work; laboratory studies show that dental fillings and mercury sensitivity can bring about a multiplicity of symptoms ranging from acute chest and back pain to thyroid enlargement and high blood pressure. Artificial and instant foods contribute to manic depression, sleeplessness, arthritis, migraine headaches and general tension.

We are presently at the mid-point between death of the old and birth of the new. We have a choice between standing still and clinging to the apparent safety of the past or taking the risk of leaping forward into the unknown. Part of us says, 'Yes, I'll jump,' but another part panics and says, 'But maybe this means I'll have to leave home, job, family.' This unconscious fear grabs us by the throat – which is where we give birth to a new identity, a new expression of ourselves – which in turn leads to mouth, throat and chest problems.

So what to do? During work with doctors who specialised in heart problems we discovered that patients who learned simple relaxation techniques recovered twice as quickly as those who did not. To learn to relax at will is a priority for perfect health. Most of us eat an over abundance of toxic, acid-forming foods. Bread (unless it's the real old-fashioned, heavy wholemeal kind), sugar, red meat, tea, coffee (especially decaffeinated), substitute butter, instant, tinned or preserved food (especially food containing monosodium glutamate), salt, most chicken and vegetable cubes, sweet desserts and puddings are therefore not good for us. To eat 80 per cent alkaline and 20 per cent acid is a good balance. To eat simple, fresh, live food – 'full-of-water' foods – will not only improve our health and immune system but will stimulate mental and physical alertness.

The Hay diet – which says don't mix starch with protein, lots of fresh fruit, vegetables and filtered water plus daily exercise – will help counteract the stress and pollution over which we have no control.

If forced to shop at bulk-buying supermarkets, once home we can deposit all our purchases in a heap and place a crystal on top for an hour or so. This will, to some extent, re-activate the life force of the food.

We can put a crystal in an airing cupboard, amongst sheets and towels or in our underwear drawers to counteract the effect of detergents and bleach.

In fact, informing ourselves and the willingness to take responsibility for how we can reduce toxicity in our lives, combined with *humour* are among the best tools we can have for mental, physical and emotional health.

Losing our minds

Insomnia, forgetfulness and emotional vulnerability are three more very common symptoms as the planet lifts to another level. We go to bed tired and yet jolt awake at 2 or 3am, as if hit by an electric shock, and then remain sleepless for the rest of the night. We go into a supermarket and forget what we came to buy, or catch a bus and find we have left the money to pay the fare at home.

In the last five years I have had problems when introducing my best friends to relative strangers. I remember the names of the strangers and forget the names of my best friends. As I stutter, stammer and blush, before mumbling, 'I can't remember your name,' everyone laughs, thinking I am being funny. I began to think I was suffering from premature senility or Alzheimer's disease and it was a great relief to realise that, even if I was, I was not alone.

Emotional vulnerability can affect us in various ways, from tears rolling down our cheeks while listening to music or watching television, to reacting in habitual ways to fears or situations we think we have overcome. Maybe our father or mother left home during our teens. We are jealous, insecure and enraged. We go out into the world, make a life for ourselves and get over the trauma when suddenly our husband, wife, or children behave in a similar way and all the old fear, anger and insecurity come to the surface again, as if the 'rusty residue' from the past needs to be cleared.

Clinical research has discovered that the food we eat can stimulate happiness or depression, mental alertness or apathy. For example we can enhance brain-power with foods rich in lecithin and glutamic acid, such as fish, wheat and soya beans. Lecithin is rich in choline, which can affect memory within ninety minutes and lasts for approximately five hours. In America researchers say that a pre-exam boost of lecithin might well improve exam results.

Ginkgo, used by the Chinese for thousands of years, has also been shown to restore memory and reverse ageing. To quote from Sheila Ostrander and Lynn Schroeder's book, *Cosmic*

Memory: 'Patients aged between sixty and eighty years old, suffering with senile dementia, were given 40mg of Ginkgo extract three times a day. In as little as eight weeks, memory and mental function were restored.' Another experiment, in which a group of young women were given Ginkgo, showed vastly improved memory and clarity of mind, with no toxic side effects.

Many doctors now say that proper nutrition can boost our intelligence as well as improve memory. Dr Linus Pauling suggests the following nutrients for top level brain function: asorbic acid, thiamine, niaicin, B6, B12, folic acid, magnesium, glutamic acid and tryptophan.

Learning from our mistakes

The replay of old events, or difficult-to-deal-with new ones, happens in order to clear the emotional or astral body. As I mentioned earlier, this body contains the imprint of everything that has happened to us, good, bad or indifferent. If we repress or deny the 'bad' or what may have been painful, it continues to affect us and will magnetise us to situations that draw the very feelings we have tried to repress to the surface. Many of us swallow our feelings – in fact lots of women gain weight around the abdomen and hips through doing just that. We 'put a good face on it', smile – sometimes through gritted teeth – and pretend things are OK when they are not. This can result not only in physical illness but also in a form of false pride which, like a glass wall, separates us from both our inner being and others.

Old emotions are triggers to past experience and if we do not deal with them once and for all we go around and around in endless circles. Only after we have dealt with them properly can we be fully and creatively conscious, and we must be that in order to participate in the changes unfolding around us. Life is now making very clear to all of us what has been hidden. It is like switching on a very bright light which shows up stains and cobwebs we never noticed before. In a similar way the violence erupting around the world does not necessarily mean things are getting worse but rather that they are becoming more visible. It is not very comfortable, so no wonder we feel vulnerable.

While some of us bury our emotions, others get as much sensation out of them as they can. Both are equally unhealthy. In the course of my work I have seen lots of people addicted to emotional sensationalism – or rather addicted to the rush of adrenalin that comes from fear, anger, hate, jealousy and so on. Even people who are constantly late frequently get an unconscious kick out of the panic to make haste. It is similar to the gambler who loses more than he wins because the adrenalin rush is greater when losing than winning. Like an addict dependent on heroin or cocaine he becomes addicted to adrenalin.

Sensationalism allows people who are stuck in their minds to get in touch with emotions they cannot contact in any other way. The thrill of being shocked by a film or play triggers a similar reaction. However, just like children who get a thrill out of being chased, or scream while playing hide and seek, we must grow out of it in order to discover real feelings.

Only then can we be clear to open up to the truth of our own lives and get in touch with our real selves, instead of being stuck in a past which we need to outgrow.

4

FOLLOWING
OUR OWN TRUTHS

Spiritual growth out of personal trauma

Shattering any illusions we have about ourselves, facing and living our own truth, is very much what the last decade of the century is about. Whether this happens through old emotions coming to the fore, or a catastrophe, it is a crucifixion of the ego. Like the crucifixion two thousand years ago it leads to transformation, pushes us to look at life from the Crown Chakra which, symbolised by the Crown of Thorns, ultimately gives a sense of equanimity and balance. It usually comes about through what we imagine is the very worst thing that could happen happening.

Obviously this is going to be different for each of us. One friend lost the use of her hands which she needed for her work as a physiotherapist; another was paralysed from the neck down after an accident. A writer with many books to his name could no longer get them published. Proud, forty-year-old parents, who had tried for years to have a child, produced a baby who was so deformed the doctors said he would never walk, talk or live a normal life.

For others this crucifixion may come through loss of wealth, work or a child. No matter how it comes we are inevitably changed afterwards. These situations pierce the persona, the shell formed by the roles we play, the structure we put around ourselves, that encloses our understanding, compassion and humanity.

When something catastrophic happens, if we can acknowledge it and then get on with life, instead of bemoaning fate or blaming God, we rob the situation of its power over us. People who blame God, or anyone else, will always be victims. They allow what has happened and other people, to dictate how they feel and what they do next.

If we could look at some of the things that happen as if they were dreams and say, 'Why? What is the message here for me? How am I meant to learn? How am I meant to change? How else could I have learned the same lesson? What is the difference in me now compared to who I was, or what I was like before?' and 'No matter if I've lost my health, my job, my wife and my friends, no matter how little there seems left, I am going to use that little to the utmost of my ability,' life suddenly co-operates with us.

A friend of mine, on the verge of finishing a thesis which had taken him ten years to formulate, returned home and found his house burned to a pile of ash, including the thesis, which he was supposed to hand in the following week. He sat beside the remains of his house for half a day, reviewing his life. With or without interpretation a phase of his life was over. He finally drove away and forced himself to rewrite what he could remember of his thesis. Instead of wasting energy on the disaster he fed it into his future. From that moment on his life took off in a new direction.

Christopher Reeve, the actor, broke his neck in a riding accident. Attractive, famous, and charismatic, Christopher appeared to be the epitome of Hollywood success and had the world at his feet. Today he is paralysed, wheelchair-bound and breathes with the help of a machine. Initially in a coma, and, when he came out of it, wanting to die, Christopher Reeve has turned his fame and fortune around and now works to publicise the plight of others who suffer crippling disability. This is true alchemy. He is also determined that one day he will walk again.

Another even more remarkable example of alchemy is that of Jean-Dominique Bauby, author of *The Diving Bell and the Butterfly*. Jean-Dominique was the debonair editor-in-chief of *Elle* magazine in Paris. One Friday evening, in December 1995, he left a meeting early in order to pick up his son and go to the theatre. Twenty days later he emerged from a coma to find an opthamologist was sewing shut his right eyelid (to prevent ulceration of the cornea). At forty-two years old, Bauby had suffered a massive stroke which had left his brain intact but his body completely paralysed – apart from a tiny movement in his left eyelid.

In *The Diving Bell and the Butterfly* he describes his condition as 'monstrous, iniquitous, revolting, terrible' – but he dictated every word of it, letter by letter, by signalling to his publishing assistant with his left eyelid. He devised his own alphabet, arranging the letters according to their frequency of use in the French language.

Every night he prepared his prose in his head and every morning Claude Mendibil, his assistant, would read each letter of his alphabet out loud and Bauby blinked when she got to the one he wanted to use. The *Daily Telegraph* describes the book as 'the most extraordinary of the year'. It was launched in March 1997 and Bauby died three days later. A book-page critique says 'the book is infused with his sharp wit – for example, "I still want to be myself – if I must drool I may as well drool on cashmere."'

Mastering our lives

One of my own personal challenges in this life has been to deal with insecurity. Sent to boarding school at six, I felt afraid, abandoned and no longer part of a family. In my late teens and early twenties I developed what I thought was a certain stability. Suddenly all my possessions – furniture, clothes, money and passport – were stolen. Within the space of eighteen months this happened three times. The first time I was so devastated I thought I would die. The second time I felt bad but knew I must pick myself up and get on with my life. The third time I shrugged my shoulders and almost laughed. I knew I was being taught that the only security worth having was an inner security not based on outer possessions.

Through these and other experiences, I thought I'd learned the lesson well. However, when it all happened again recently I suddenly realised I was not as immune as I thought I was. Feeling violated and insecure, I wept. When a friend told me to thank the people who had done this to me, and who therefore helped release me from attachment to material possessions, I wanted to smack her in the face, even though I knew what she said was true.

My sense of abandonment at the age of six came up again through many friends and acquaintances gradually disappearing out of my life – either through death, moving to another place or simply drifting into other things. This shifting kaleidoscopic pattern of people coming together and moving apart is nowadays a common occurrence. It will increase in the future. It is as if invisible strings are pulling us together with people we either have to learn something from, do something with or are part of our soul family.

There is usually a feeling of instant recognition, a compatibility and 'knowing' of each other, even if, in this life, we have never met before. On some other plane we saw the script, even helped to write it, had a dress rehearsal and now the curtain is rising and the play is about to start.

An actor in a theatre moves on to the stage and plays his part to the best of his ability. If he carried with him thoughts of all the people in his life who are not on stage with him at this particular moment he would forget his lines. It is the same for us. If we can live in the moment, value whoever or whatever is in our life today and bless and release them when they go, we can participate fully in our part in the play and not get stuck in loneliness and self-pity.

Obviously this is not always easy to do but it is something to aim towards and leaves us as 'masters' of the events of our lives, rather than victimised by them. Then even defeat caused by our own conscious sins and omissions can lead us to say, in the words of Ashleigh Brilliant, 'I've learned so much from my failures that I'm thinking of having some more.'

The influence of Pluto

This process, which kills off past behaviour patterns and strips us of our old identities and props, is partly due to the influence of Pluto. Pluto rules elimination and regeneration; reflects the power of knowing when to hold on and when to let go, symbolises descent into the underworld, the downward spiral of spirit into matter. Plutonian energy stimulates self-confrontation, stirs us to face our own shadow – the repressed, neurotic, traumatised or unlived part of ourselves. This confrontation breaks down, and can break through, the crystallisation of old fears and taboos – another way of describing the crucifixion of the ego.

After confrontation or descent, which puts the personality in crisis, comes rebirth. The personality in difficulty behaves like a drowning man who, at his strongest the moment before death, is likely to attack his saviour, or grasp at any straw, in order to save himself. That straw may be drugs, alcohol or holding on to past bad habits. We can be destroyed by keeping Pluto's energy in check or we can use it to go through transition and rebirth; we can own, misuse or deny our own power.

In the past two or three years I have seen many people descend into the underworld, not always voluntarily, to find an aspect of themselves that has shocked both them and others. For example a woman who had previously led a 'blameless', somewhat passive life, catering to the needs of everyone around her and ignoring her own, suddenly began secretly to shoplift, while at home she expressed herself in increasingly violent temper tantrums. Whatever we repress we feed with energy. Finally it erupts like a pressure-cooker exploding. This woman had learned in childhood from an alcoholic, and frequently enraged, father that losing your temper or being honest about needs and wants was something you just did not do. It was not 'nice', it caused problems.

Pluto now forces us to admit the truth about ourselves, acknowledge what we truly feel, and accept that we are the sum total of many parts, 'good' and 'bad'. Once we integrate them, they no longer have hidden power over us.

It is partly Pluto's influence which has shattered the façade of the British Royal Family. Anything corrupt, criminal, phoney or false – such as the Maxwell Empire, the Vatican Bank and dealings by some Italian politicians with the Mafia – is likely to be under tremendous pressure. Some of the major scandals blazoned in newspaper headlines across the world for us all to see are simply archetypal reflections of what lie in our own unconscious. Instead of pointing a critical finger at some of these situations we need to examine what may be phoney or false in our own lives and do something about it.

The next twenty years will see the structure of many established institutions which are not based on absolute truth crumble and collapse. Some of them are already beginning to do so.

In May 1997 I received the following note from Petra Du Preez, a well known South African astrologer:

> The movements of Uranus, Neptune and Pluto are of interest to astrologers since these mark periods of humankind's evolution on a collective level . . . Pluto, the planet of transformation, necessitates a symbolic death and rebirth process. It requires that we strip away and let go of that which is old, outdated and no longer of use for future growth. It compels us individually and collectively with an urge to break through the taboos of society, to bring forth and challenge the validity of hitherto hidden issues. Educational, religious and ethical issues will be explored to their core so that a new order can emerge, based not on our inherited values but on values reflecting our changing society.

Petra also said that Uranus moved into Aquarius during 1996, and will stimulate enormous change in our world view, social awareness and understanding of our inter-relatedness. My understanding of these words is that we will have access to information that pushes us far beyond the concept of a global village and choices that reflect the interdependent nature of life on Earth to a recognition of our inter-connectedness with and to other planetary civilisations.

Synchronicity

1992 in particular, especially the months of April, May and June, was a year in which we had our masks stripped off. Time, space, spirit and matter merged together. Synchronicity and instant manifestation became increasingly common.

Synchronicity, a term coined by Jung, implies 'clusters of significant events occurring together'. For example, I may think of something, switch on the radio and hear an announcer simultaneously saying the very words I am thinking, or I may think of a friend and a second later he or she telephones, or knocks on my door.

Instant manifestation is an aspect of synchronicity. Whatever you need in the moment appears. Sometimes these may seem like very small, trivial coincidences, but once you start acknowledging them, you will find yourself opening up to the magic in your life. Recently, for instance, while travelling, I discovered I had left my toothpaste behind. In a hotel bathroom, with no immediate means of replacing it, I began to clean my teeth with soap when I suddenly found a half-empty tube left by another guest. Buying a takeaway Chinese meal I realised I had nothing to eat it with. Wishing for a spoon I suddenly found one in the grass under my feet. (Whether I used it or not is another matter! The point is that the universe provided.)

Today synchronicity also means instant karma – karma is the law of cause and effect. I express impatience with a person and five minutes later receive the same treatment from someone else. I see, but do not tell, that the checkout girl in the supermarket has given me too much change. As I place my purchases in the car, my bag is stolen. When time, space, spirit and matter merge it is a little like being in the still, clear centre of a cyclone where there is no time, no space. Every now and again we are spun out and everything stops – as if we were in a time warp between dimensions.

This is partly why we become increasingly forgetful and nothing makes sense! I do not know who I am, who you are, or what I am meant to be doing! I go upstairs to get my purse or coat, or to clean the bath and stand mesmerised, wondering why

I am standing at the top of the stairs. I write a list to make sure this does not happen again but when I need it the list disappears. So do most other things when I need them. The letter I not only wrote but stamped and addressed is not where I left it when I go to the post office. The keys I know I put in my coat pocket reappear – two days later – under my pillow. So called inanimate objects apparently stroll about day and night, changing positions so they are never where I think they are, only to return when I have long given up hope of ever finding them again. When I was a child my Irish grandmother said it was because of the gremlins. If so the gremlins are now teasing us all.

The conjunction of Uranus, Neptune and Capricorn

When I first wrote this book, Uranus and Neptune were coming together in Capricorn, which meant that 1993 promised to be one of the most potent times in the awakening of mass consciousness and the history of human evolution. It was the seed point in the change of our beliefs and attitudes, and led into a crisis of values and a breakdown of the old systems. The consequences of this breakdown could be seen through the Middle East, South Africa, Bosnia, the former USSR, and Cambodia. The year 1993 introduced a new beginning where man was stripped of his illusions and started to take control of what he knew.

The discovery of Uranus, the rule-breaker, heralded new ways of thinking, coincided with the American and French Revolutions and the beginning of the Industrial Revolution. Uranus inspires us to break away from mass-conditioning to search for individuality, a new world and enlightenment. Neptune, the mystical planet, governs dreams, fantasy, illusion, psychic phenomena, the astral plane and stimulates telepathy and channelling. The recognition of Neptune as a planet heralded the use of ether as an anaesthetic, hypnotism, magic lantern shows as a prelude to the fantasy of the cinema, romantic literature and art, and many other forms of escapism.

Uranus and Neptune in Capricorn signified an increase of earth and weather changes, as part of the process of cleansing as well as revolutionary changes in government and other organisations which will ultimately produce a more humanitarian attitude to all of life.

To deal with these changes we need to be fully awake and able to move beyond the limitations of our own consciousness. It is therefore also significant that, in addition to the conjunction of Uranus and Neptune in Capricorn, we were at my first writing – February 1993 – entering the Chinese year of the Cosmic Rooster. Just as a live rooster heralds the dawn of a new day, so did the energies of the Cosmic Rooster accelerate our awakening.

In numerology, the science of numbers, 1993 adds up to 22. Twenty-two is known as a Master number which brings added potential for self-mastery and the opportunity to realise our unlimited potential. Twenty-two adds up to four which is a number of mastering the laws of the Earth, of balancing mind, body, emotion and spirit, of bringing all things into order. The two numbers twenty-two and four symbolise the concept of Heaven on Earth, or the linking of cosmic consciousness to planet Earth. It is a blending of the mystical with the practical.

The conjunction of Neptune, Uranus and Capricorn continued to affect us into 1994 and 1995. This conjunction, as it moves through the 1990s, stimulates, on the one hand, the recognition of our need for co-operation, communication and community, while on the other reminds us of our differences. We shall have the choice between saying: 'These differences are so great that we cannot live together' or to turning ourselves upside down in trying to see things from another point of view. If we take fixed attitudes and refuse to unbend we could see a world at war. The choice will virtually be co-operation or obliteration. As W. H. Auden wrote, 'we must love one another or die'.

Planetary alignments into the twenty-first century

According to Roy Gillett, a well-known astrologer (whose address I include at the end of the book), the planetary alignments of the 1990s bring confrontation between the forces of ignorance and the forces of enlightenment. He says we have a lot of hard work to do, both individually and collectively: we must face and overcome our karmic lessons and become stable, centred and disciplined. The late 1990s will push us to face one challenge after another until we recognise that the one true solution to all our problems is to deal with their causes rather than with their symptoms.

Roy told me that 1997 has produced a general appetite for change but that in 1998, when Neptune moves into Aquarius, we will believe in a different future. He says that fashion and religion will take on a 'zany, humanitarian techno perspective' and that 1997–2012 should see belief in new technology, distribution of knowledge and energy as well as enlightened attitudes. He believes that the new millennium will not start on 1 January 2000 but rather a year later, and that 1999 could be a difficult year of confrontation with tests of love, compassion and responsibility.

A group of astrologers in America, known as the 'Star Fire Group' have analysed the Book of Revelation according to the predicted movements of the planets. They suggest that 1998 brings with it several significant star events. As Pluto moves towards Antares, the heart of the Scorpion, on 26 February 1998, a total eclipse of the sun is due to take place. A similar solar eclipse on the same date nineteen years earlier in 1979 signalled the onset of apocalyptic signs in the Heavens and on Earth. Its repetition will mark a critical period and turning point for humanity. Each human being will be confronted with a conscious decision: 'Do I follow the lamb or the beast?'

At the end of this century there will be a major configuration of planets, a configuration that takes place once in a lifetime or approximately every sixty years. The Star Fire Group traced this conjunction back in history to AD 34, when they say there was a similar conjunction at the time of St Paul's conversion. This brings to mind that humanity will face a similar opportunity for conversion, and that it is this that will herald in the golden age of the twenty-first century predicted by so many throughout the world.

In any case, the current and future combination of stars, planets, signs, symbols and portents promise that no matter what problems we may face now – personal or planetary – we really will see a change of consciousness that reconnects us to our own divinity, our own perfection, and enables us to become a part of the universal brotherhood of enlightened humanity.

Paul Panos, a South African friend who describes himself as 'a student of ageless wisdom, with an interest in astrology', rather than a full-time astrologer, has the following comments to make on the planetary influences as we move towards the next millennium: '. . . the religious movements of the world are likely to be placed under intense self-scrutiny and unprecedented change . . . which could catalyse a new world religion.' He says that the result of Uranus entering Aquarius in 1996 was illumination, innovation and change. In his words, 'Uranus rules the intuition so those who are able to exercise this faculty are likely to come to the forefront – females in general being the more intuitive of genders are likely to play a more important role . . . The conjunction of Neptune with Uranus, while transiting the final degrees of Capricorn, could also be the reason why we are trying to curb, on a global scale, drugs, alcoholism, smoking and destructive self-indulgence.

In January 1998 Neptune enters Aquarius and will remain in conjunction with Uranus until August 1998 but will still be in Aquarius as the year 2000 ends. Paul says that with this combination the world could come up with real solutions to some of the problems that beset humanity. He adds: 'Since authoritarianism is a vestige of the waning Piscean influences, the dictatorial executive in Beijing could find itself facing insurmountable pressure to liberalise . . . during Pluto's reign in Sagittarius, legislative bodies around the world may be more inclined to create laws and policies which take into greater account both the material and spiritual well-being of the individual . . . not least of all there could be an intensified pursuit for higher knowledge, and an almost unquenchable thirst for truth . . .'.

Paul Panos says the most significant development in modern astrology is its move away from prediction to deep spiritual and psychological guidance. He adds, 'the growth in numbers of astrological students in the world today is nothing short of astronomical – there are tens of thousands of students and thousands of teachers. The demystification of astrology has made it more accessible to other disciplines and is often used as a diagnostic tool and guide in the medical profession; in psychiatry; for validation by archaeologists and astronomers, as well as for projections by futurists.'

I am not an astrologer, although I have a passionate belief in how the interaction of planetary energies influence my life. I *have* found it useful to think of each astrological sign as one of the colleges in the school curriculum of life. In other words, the lessons of Aries are to do with identity, I am; Taurus, I have; Gemini, I think; Cancer, I feel; Leo, I will; Virgo, I analyse; Libra, I harmonise; Scorpio, I desire; Sagittarius, I perceive; Capricorn, I use; Aquarius, I serve; and Pisces, we integrate.

The first four signs are self-oriented; the second four are interpersonal (i.e. they consider other people to be of equal importance as themselves); the next four are extra-personal, more interested in the world around them, even – in the case of Aquarius and Pisces – to the point of impersonal self-sacrifice.

During the course of many lives we will deal with the challenges all these colleges of life provide. In addition, each one relates to an element of Fire, Earth, Air and Water which also influence our lives.

Planets of fire are: *Aries, Leo and Sagittarius*. When balanced, Fire people are assertive, strong and dynamic. When unbalanced, they are easily angry (hot under the collar), and tend to blame others for all that goes wrong.

Planets of Earth are: *Taurus, Virgo and Capricorn*. When balanced, they are practical, steadfast (loyal) and centred. Unbalanced, they are stodgy, stick in the muds, a bit boring.

Air signs are: *Gemini, Libra and Aquarius*. In balance they are joyful, light and humorous. Out of balance, they can be flakey, flighty and irrelevant (i.e. they don't listen or they change the conversation away from the subject discussed).

Water signs (*Pisces, Cancer and Scorpio*) are all signs of almost psychic sensitivity to the needs of others. When balanced they are loyal, loving and nurturing. Out of balance their fear of hurt can lead to loneliness which then appears as cold. They hide their feelings, close up verbally, fear exposure and resist being pushed by others.

Today's astrology for the individual is more like a soul-centred psychological road map which charts opportunities, strengths, weaknesses, challenges, and points out where a person's major focus should be in terms of work, relationships, etc.

No matter what astrological sign or college we are enrolled in, nor what chakra level or Earth element we function from, connection to our higher or soul selves is the key to following our own truths fearlessly. We can make this connection through meditation, dreams or imagination. For example, imagine going into a house and down to the cellar or basement to find your lower self first. This lower self can appear as an unhappy or irresponsible child who needs love and attention before you bring it up to the ground floor to find your conscious self. Now imagine entering the kitchen or living room, even the garden, and call the conscious self to reveal itself to you and introduce it to the lower self, or child. Allow time for them to meet and then take them to the top of the house or outside to a wood or hill where your higher self will be waiting for you. This can often produce better results than just looking for the higher self on its own. Once you have made contact with these other selves, you may like to connect with the soul or higher self in a more sacred spiritual setting of your own preference.

5

LEARNING FROM THE MYTHS AND PROPHECIES OF THE PAST

The lesson of Atlantis

It was my first visit to America. I arrived in New York after thirty-six hours of sleeping with my fellow passengers on the pavement outside the airline building, owing to a strike by aircraft personnel. Tired, crumpled and unwashed, I was nevertheless stunned by the throb of the city and the vast, red-orange, rising sun which, like a huge Christmas-tree bauble, seemed to dangle among the soaring skyscraper buildings.

I decided to go immediately to the Empire State Building where I felt I could communicate with and talk to the Angel of New York. (I believe that each home, city and country has its own guiding, angelic force and that by communicating with this presence – greeting it when you arrive, thanking it when you leave, the place you live in, or visit, reveals itself to you in a different way.) From the Empire State Building I went to the Statue of Liberty and then on to the Meditation Room on the ground floor of the United Nations.

Having aligned myself with what I believe are three key energy points in New York, I began to have extraordinary visions of tidal waves engulfing the city. I saw what appeared to be Atlantis in its latter days – a shimmering silver city where men like gods flew through the air, over and under the sea, across and through the Earth. If this sounds far-fetched, think of modern aeroplanes, submarines, trains, buses and underground trains. The Atlanteans were a highly advanced civilisation who knew how to tap the energy of the universe; who understood how to harness the energy of the sun through giant and carefully placed crystals. They used the resulting rays for heat and light (just as we use electricity today); for communication – similar to our telephone, radio and television; the development of psychic powers such as telepathy and clairvoyance; the transport of heavy objects; the invention of atomic power as well as the rejuvenation of ailing or deformed bodies (not unlike modern laser treatment). Even organ transplants were common at this time.

All over the world stories of Atlantis abound. Many of them have been written about in books, much has come from psychics and clairvoyants sharing their visions, while others have been passed from generation to generation by word of mouth. One of the first books to mention Atlantis was Plato's *Timaeus*, written in the fifth century BC, in which Plato describes a conversation between a number of Egyptian priests and Solon, an Athenian statesman. These priests talk about Atlantis as a great island known as Poseida which existed as a vast continent between what we now know as eastern America and western Europe. They said it had been a powerful kingdom but because of the wickedness of its inhabitants it was destroyed.

Both Atlantis and its predecessor, Lemuria – or Mu – were founded on the Law of One; the belief in, the worship and love of, one God. As the Lemurians and Atlanteans moved away from this into the worship of science, power and material possessions, their civilisations began to fall apart. War, poverty, hunger, sexual indulgence and perversion were widespread.

As I looked across New York from the Empire State Building I was completely unaware of Plato, Voltaire, Montaigne, Buffon and Francis Bacon, who have all written about Atlantis. I simply had a sense of the destruction of a so-called 'perfect-race' brought about by their refusal to recognise and acknowledge the power of God, of nature and each other. In that moment I felt that we of this century are all reborn Atlanteans. We are presented with similar circumstances, have the opportunity to choose between construction or destruction, the brotherhood of man or the domination by one race or group of another. Also like the Atlanteans, who were given many warnings, we know change is coming but we are not willing to do anything about it.

Much of Atlantean technology supposedly came from extra-terrestrials or beings from outer space who, according to a number of psychics, freely visited the Earth at this time. These space visitors helped design the giant crystals which, in the beginning, were a tremendous force for good. However, finally, through their gross misuse, enormous explosions were set off, devastating the land, causing earthquakes and tidal waves which washed the Atlantean civilisation off the face of the Earth. Before these cataclysms took place, wise men and uncorrupt priests, taking their psychic and scientific knowledge with them, began to lead small groups of people away from Atlantis to settle in different parts of the world. There they established schools in which mathematics, astronomy, engineering, writing and worship of the law of One were taught.

Recent channelled messages from American psychics state that power and light began to be withdrawn from the Crystal Grid System in the Earth long before the Atlantean misuse of crystals destroyed their civilisation. This took place on the continent of Lemuria. Priests who sensed what was happening tried to reactivate the grid for spiritual use while others tried to manipulate it for greed. Like Atlantis, Lemuria eventually broke apart and sank. A part of it became the land we know as Australia.

According to these readings, the Aboriginal men of know-ledge have known throughout time of their ancient origins and also that they would eventually play a part in the reactivation of the grid. This would be done by sound transmitted through a 40,000-year-old wind instrument – the didgeridoo. Although different groups, both incarnate and discarnate, have been directing energy and light into the Earth and its crystal grid system for many years, it was during the 1996 Olympic Games that the final healing took place. The sound of the didgeridoo, played during the closing ceremonies of the Games, was heard by over four billion people worldwide. As they listened, they were aligned with each other as well as with Mother Earth. At this moment the final stage of re-energising the grid took place. As light expanded through the crystal grid system it is said that the force of cosmic evil was shattered and planet Earth was freed to lift into another level. By a strange – or maybe not so strange – coincidence, on the day this occurred the Unity Church Daily Word reading said: 'Today I break the bonds of negativity and clear the way for harmony.'

When I lived in America, I met many groups who gathered in expectation of 'Ascension' or 'the Rapture'. They tended to believe they were especially chosen and would be lifted up by space craft while the rest of us, who were not good enough or evolved enough, would be left behind to suffer days of darkness. I personally believe that words such as Ascension or Rapture simply imply the quantum leap of consciousness that is predicted to take place during the next ten years. Everyone will, in effect, 'wake up' to the knowlege of who they truly are – some, perhaps, through death and others through meditation and expanded spiritual awareness. A few, though not all, of these groups now feel that maybe Ascension occurred when the crystal grid activation was completed.

Patti Diane Cota-Robles (*The New Age Study of Humanity's Purpose*) believes that this moment freed humanity from its karma. She says: 'We still have free will. We still have our human egos and we still have the ability to "misqualify" our thoughts, words, actions and feelings to recreate chaos in our lives. But if we choose not to, if we choose to revere our gift of life and use our creative faculties to add to the Light of the World, we can transform our lives into expressions of joy, love, abundance, happiness and every other expression of Divinity we desire.'

Cayce's readings on Atlantis

According to the Cayce readings, the destruction of Lemuria and Atlantis took place in three different phases with many years in-between. The final one was a cataclysm so great that the world's topography was changed in an instant. Cold countries became hot, hot countries froze in the twinkling of an eye. This instant change of climate brought death to thousands of people as well as to many of the enormous animals, such as dinosaurs, that roamed the Earth at that time.

Edgar Cayce believed this destruction came during a time when the Earth shifted on its axis and that this would happen again before the end of this century. He also predicted the reappearance of parts of Atlantis in the form of islands rising out of the sea off the American coast. Many psychics have pinpointed the Bermuda Triangle as the area in which the giant crystal, whose powerful rays helped to cause this pole-shift, lies. This is also an area where hundreds of people have inexplicably disappeared without trace as if the crystal rays are still alive.

During a seminar in Greece, I had a vision in which I saw the sparkling silver and gold cities of Atlantis. Domed temples and gleaming, sky-scraper-like buildings arose from gardens filled with the fragrance of brilliantly coloured flowers, the sound of birds and the tinkle and splash of water from streams and waterfalls. People, many of whom appeared to be hundreds of years old, bathed in vibrationally charged water or sat in geometric patterns of crystals and light, to maintain their health and vitality. Special herbs and plants were grown, essences designed for spiritual upliftment while gem elixirs helped to balance etheric dysfunction.

Technology appeared to be far in advance of our present day scientific developments. Cloning, transplants, in-vitro fertilisation and genetic manipulation that mixed animal and human cells, were an accepted use of life-force. Telepathy and clairvoyance, the ability to read – and even enter – the Akashic records, enabled the Atlanteans to communicate with life – past, present and future. Colour, sound, crystals – all forms of electromagnetic energy, were used to stimulate creativity and mental genius.

Edgar Cayce predicted that many of us in this century are reincarnated Atlanteans and that much information about Atlantis would surface during our lives. It is therefore not surprising that we talk about energy medicine and vibrational healing. An example of this is Radionics, which believes that each organ and disease has its own vibrational frequency which can be treated after assessing the mental, physical and emotional state of the patient, the Ray for which he functions, his chakra balance, as well as the subtle energy fields around him. Today many other forms of vibrational healing are popping up, all of which seem based on ancient Atlantean healing techniques.

World myths

During the past twenty years I have travelled extensively in many countries, including Africa, Egypt, Australia, America and New Zealand. I have spoken to Maoris, Aboriginals, American Indians and African witch doctors. Their stories seem to coincide, overlap and corroborate each other. Stories about people who travelled to the far corners of the Earth and who became the foundation of the black, white, brown, yellow and red races. Information handed down by word of mouth has become the stuff of legend, myth and fantasy. It cannot surely be coincidence that so many cultures share the same myths. I believe they possibly originated in Atlantis.

It is not only indigenous people who share these memories. Paco Rabanne, the world famous designer, claimed in a recent *Evening Standard* interview that he survived banishment from the Crystal Planet, witnessed the fall of Atlantis and was swept away in the flood. He described coming to Earth with sixty companions on a flying saucer to build a settlement that would eventually become Atlantis. He said that initially Atlantis was cold so they decided to use huge, energy-emitting crystals to change the weather and make it warmer. The crystals turned out to be more powerful than the scientists expected and caused the Earth to turn on its axis.

The Hopi prophecies

I wish I had known of Paco Rabanne's beliefs before I went to America because for many months after my initial visit to New York, no matter where I went, I had images of Atlantis and walls of water rising around me and began to doubt my sanity. I had a sense of what it must have felt like to have been swallowed up by a great wave of water. Then I read an article by a Cherokee

American Indian physicist who described a life of being one of the Star people and how these memories fit together with many tribal legends. He said:

> We lived in domed cities with translucent walls. We could fly, communicate with animals, transport ourselves instantly to other parts of the world. I remember our city as a golden colour – a place of great beauty and calm. I came with others from my planet to help Earth through its birth pains into an intergalactic community and oneness. We were members of the priestcraft in Ancient Egypt; alchemists in the Middle Ages; scientists and clergy in the modern world.

Like many other native Americans or American Indians, he believes that there has been a close interaction between humans and the Star People, even to the point of having children, and that our current problems are caused by separation from the stars. In fact, the word 'dis-aster' means 'separation from the stars'.

Inspired by his words, I decided to explore more American Indian myths and legends. I found that most of them tell of previous worlds in which humanity reached great heights of culture and creativity but failed to honour the Mother Earth on which they lived or to acknowledge the teachings of the Great Spirit.

In 1970, Hopi Chief Dan Katchongua said, 'The Hopis were survivors of another world that was destroyed by flood.' Rolling Thunder, a Cherokee medicine priest, also talked about ancient civilisations, pyramids, prophecies, UFOs, Atlantis and what people can do now to prepare for coming events.

According to Hopi mythology, the universe was created by TAIOWA, the infinite creative force. In the beginning, all were attuned to the infinite. However, they gradually lost this connection and forgot their origins. According to Hopi elders, people 'lost the use of the vibratory centre at the top of the head, and the soft spot that was the doorway between the body and the spirit began to harden'. TAIOWA decided that this was not permissible so, while saving some people who were taken to the centre of the Earth, he/she ordered the destruction of the world.

In this legend, the North and South Poles shifted, resulting in an Ice Age. Hopi myths talk of people travelling in flying machines, but when they began to use them for war, TAIOWA sent waves taller than mountains to sweep over the land. Those who were faithful to the ancient teachings of the Great White Spirit became 'the Chosen People' and were sealed into hollow tubes so they could float upon the water. This sounds very similar to the story of Noah's Ark.

The Hopi prophecies talk about the 'True White Brother' who will come as the day of purification approaches. He will bring with him sacred stone tablets, matching the ones given by the Great White Spirit after the last time of destruction. These tablets contain teachings, instructions and prophecies.

To enable the Hopi leaders to check when the return of the True White Brother is imminent, certain signs and events were predicted. One was that white men would bring wagons hooked to each other and pulled by something other than a horse. Trains fulfilled this prophecy. They were shown roads in the sky, cobwebs in the air and lines across the land. These prophecies were fulfilled, the Hopi say, by airline routes, vapour trails, highways, electricity and telephone wires.

They were told that a 'gourd of ashes' would cause great destruction and believe this was the atomic bomb. Yet another prediction was that two brothers would 'build a ladder' to the moon – the moon landing – and that one of the last signs would be when man put his house in the sky. This could be the Skylab Space Laboratory that fell. After that the time of great changes would be near. Prophecies for three major world events are inscribed on rock and a sacred gourd rattle used in Hopi ceremonies.

One is the swastika, the other the sun and the third the colour red. The swastika symbolised Germany in World War II; the sun Japan and World War II. The colour red has yet to manifest but the Hopi believe that when the third sign comes it will either be complete rebirth or total annihilation. The choice is ours and depends on our balancing ourselves, changing our consciousness and living in harmony with each other and the Earth.

So seriously did the wise men and leaders of the Hopi take

these prophecies that when they saw them come to pass they decided they had a responsibility to share them with the world. In 1948 and 1973 they went to the United Nations but were rejected. In 1976, in Canada, at a UN sponsored conference, they were finally allowed to deliver their message. This message basically asks us to honour the Earth as a sacred, living being who loves us like a mother and who, also like a mother, gives us a big shake when we behave badly.

The native Americans feel they are keepers and protectors of the land – especially the American continent. However, each tribe or nation has a particular duty. For example, Hopi means 'peaceful people' – 'those who follow a peaceful path'. They never fought white men, continue in a traditional way to live on the land, farming and grazing cattle – trying to blend *with* nature rather than conquer her.

The Cherokees' prophecies

The Cherokees, known as the Principal People, understood the power of sound and crystallography. Cherokee means 'people who speak a strange tongue'. They have kept a fire, which they say, like their ancestors, came from the stars. They think of all mankind as Star People who came to Earth from Sirius. This is also the belief of the Dogon tribe in NW Africa – see Robert Temple's *The Sirius Mystery*. Dhyani Ywahoo, a medicine woman and Cherokee princess, told me that she was taught by her grandfather that, even when her people were forced to hide in caves, this fire was carefully carried and tended.

Native Americans – like most other indigenous peoples – feel they have a spiritual responsibility for the environment. They believe that we are given the opportunity of life in order to recognise 'the Great Mystery' or the 'One' from whom we all descend. This means to live in step with the seasons, attuned to the Sun and the cycles of the Moon, and, through these rhythms, interact with the Earth and the universe.

In Dhyani Ywahoo's book, *Voices of our Ancestors*, she talks about an ideal life where we can honour and respect one another. She talks about 'this time of purification' and suggests we can manifest the ideal as follows:

First affirm that there's a path of beauty, very diligently put your feet upon that path, and with great energy, through the practice of good voice, speak of what is good, recognise what is, and what may be, in the process of change. When speaking of something that needs correction, let the energy you place upon it within your voice be without charge, that things may come to balance and resolution ... By practising a voice of compassion, by activating the wisdom that discriminates, we can speak to one another in the moment and realise how to work together. Basically, as human beings, we wish to survive and to communicate with one another. We are all coming to know, in a deeper way, the nature of true communication. It is said that there will be a time when all upon this planet will speak one language and that language will be few words, many visions. That is a seed germinating in our hearts even now.

The Cherokees were renowned for their ability to heal with crystals. They still revere their crystal skulls which were known to sing and speak. These skulls were supposed to hold prophetic information about life, programmed into them in the same way that we store memory in computers today.

Like the Hopis, Dhyani also spoke of the 'Pale One' or 'Keeper of Mysteries', who not only came when people forgot their spiritual duties in the past, but will come again to 'rekindle the sacred fire', or share the teachings that will help humanity develop. Ancient prophecies, previously kept secret in order to protect them, and handed down by word of mouth, ceremony and ritual, are now being revealed to help us prepare for this time.

'The Rainbow Woman'

Brooke Medicine Eagle is from the Nez Perce and Sioux clans in North America. She did her ritual training with a Cheyenne medicine woman and earned a BA in psychology and mathematics, and a Master's degree in counselling psychology at the University of Denver. She later gave up on Western education and now devotes herself to the sacred ways of her people. She believes that the dreams and visions of Black Elk, and many other Native American seers and wise men and women, are now coming true. Brooke Medicine Eagle's own vision was given to her by someone she refers to as 'the Rainbow Woman'. In it she was told that the Earth is in trouble and the people on it are out of balance. 'We need to put more emphasis on surrendering, being receptive, allowing, nurturing,' says Brooke Medicine Eagle. 'Women especially need to find their place, to find the strength of their place, and that also the whole society, men and women, need that balance to bring ourselves into balance.'

Brooke Medicine Eagle believes she is the bridge between two cultures, the old and the new, the Indian and the present white dominant one. She says, 'The Indian people are the people of the heart. When the white man came to this land what he was to bring was the intellect, that analytical, intellectual way of being. And the Indians were to develop the heart, the feeling. And those two were to come together to build the new age, in balance, not one or the other. In the philosophy of the true Indian people, Indian is an attitude, a state of mind; Indian is a state of being, the place of the heart.'

Books such as *Fingerprints of the Gods, Keeper of Genesis, The Orion Mystery* and *The Sirius Connection*, in which archaeology, geology, astrology and astronomy reveal connections between various civilisations since the last Ice Age and before, have gripped the minds and imagination of men and women with almost no previous interest in historical facts. An image of a pyramid on television, in a magazine or displayed in a travel agent's window can trigger hours of discussion on whether the Sphinx will reveal its secrets before the year 2000, as predicted by Edgar Cayce. *The Hiram Key*, the David Icke series of books which include *The Robots' Rebellion*, and *Secret Societies and their Power in the 20th Century*, by Jan van Helsing, push us to take responsibility for our lives.

The most amazing contribution to learning from myths and prophecies of the past was, for me, the words I heard spoken by one of the Cherokee crystal skulls during a channelling session. The 'voice' was so funny that one of the group I was working with asked, 'Why do you speak like that?' The skull replied 'I am doing the best I can.' It went on to say that a crystal skull 'vibrates thought from words' and that we can access the knowledge implanted within it through love, and the belief that communication is possible. When asked where it came from, the skull said it was pre-Mayan Atlantean, pre Lemurian. It claimed to be more than 81,000 years old but it added that this could not be compared with the concept of time on planet Earth as we did not understand 'simultaneous time'.

One person asked if there was life on other planets, and if there was a civilisation inside the Earth. The skull replied, 'Affirmative to both questions.' There was a long silence and it then went on to say there were forms of life on every planet in the universe but because their vibration was different we did not see them. The skull said nothing was dead, everything existed in its own vibrational frequency.

When questioned about God, the skull answered, 'The Creator, that which you term God, is beyond comprehension. Air, Earth, stars, oceans, a slab of concrete, the chair you sit on – all is God. Don't limit by a name. All that is *is*, with no concept of good, bad or evil. Man is not separate from, but symbiotic with, all that is – is an expression of God consciousness and, through different levels of consciousness, interplays with all dimensions.'

The skull explained that information and intelligence had been implanted into it, and other skulls, by thought projection. We could use this knowledge now if we were willing to bring 'knowledge into action' and move beyond fear. It said that all minds are inter-connected and if we could re-programme our minds away from fear, express and be peace, and share love, humanity's consciousness would instantly change.

Someone asked if it was right to continue with the space programme. The skull said, 'Yes. Continue to move forward and outward *but* look at your intent, your motivation. If you explore to conquer, no, it is not right.' Another questioner asked, 'Are some people on Earth descendants of other realities and if so, why don't we now find traces of these other realities?' The skull said there were traces but so far they were undiscovered. He also said that thought transformation, the use of high frequencies, allowed space travel and could also move, change, and elevate objects. (I imagine this to refer to some of the huge stones in sacred sites such as Stonehenge.)

Over and over again, the skull repeated the need to love self and then others, in order to transform the world and survive into the future. To flow with the energy and vibration of love, to move beyond any barriers created by fear, allows us to be at one with and receive healing from all of creation.

The Mayan Calendar and the Harmonic Convergence

The Mayan Calendar, deciphered by Jose Arguelles, says that the 'tide went out' in 3113 BC and will not return until midnight on Christmas Eve AD 2011. The Mayan Calendar came to an end in 1987 but predicted the importance of the years between 1987 and 2012. In order to share this information world-wide, Jose Arguelles inaugurated the Harmonic Convergence in 1987. This was a global celebration where thousands of people gathered together to honour the end of the world as we have known it, the end of Mayan timekeeping, and to welcome the new era coming in.

This is also a wonderful thing to do at the end of one year and the beginning of the next. To thank the old year, no matter what it brought into our lives, to then bless and release it, frees us, leaves us empty and open to greet the new year and the new opportunities it will bring. When the Harmonic Convergence took place, I was in South Africa. We planted a tree both for peace and to acknowledge the seeding of a new consciousness, a new understanding, taking root. To know that all over the world, at that moment, thousands of other trees were being planted for the same purpose, gave us all a sense of planetary connection.

A time of awakening

The Mayan Calendar states categorically that 2011 will see the birth of a new consciousness in the world and return to a time of trust and innocence.

This is not unlike the current expectation of people who await the Second Coming, the return of Jesus, Buddha, or the Maitreya, the rebirth of the Christ, the days of Rapture, the return of the Eternals, or the Peacemaker or Star People, who will descend from starry constellations to save us.

Throughout history we have gazed at the heavens searching for signs of life. Although most indigenous tribes believe they came from the stars – the Australian Aboriginals trace themselves to a race from the Seven Sisters, the constellation known as the Pleiades (others call this the Seven Dancers) – until recently most of us have dismissed such ideas as ridiculous. Now, after books by such writers as Von Daniken and Velikovsky, dramatic sightings of UFOs and supposed messages from outer space, even scientists are willing to take a second look.

The Aboriginals say they are still in communication with their brothers in the sky – in fact they too are awaiting the arrival of a new Star brother or sister who will help reshape their world. Aside from numerous claims from space-contactees that, not only have they been befriended by extra-terrestrials, but have also had joy-rides in a variety of spacecraft – which sometimes led to physical examination and sexual contact – there are also a number of men and women who claim to be psychic channels of information, fed to them telepathically, from outer space. Others have had personal 'on-the-ground' meetings with space people. One such well-known meeting was between Arthur Henry Matthews, a friend of Nikola Tesla, the electrical genius, and two golden-haired, blue-eyed men who said they were from Venus. They had come to see what Matthews was doing with Tesla's unpatented inventions. When Matthews expressed disbelief they said, 'When you see our ship you will believe.'

The leader drew from memory a sketch of an anti-war machine which only Matthews and Tesla knew about. Finally convinced, Matthews went with them and climbed aboard their craft. He was amazed to discover it was controlled by mind-power. In most cases of extra-terrestrial contact the messages have been of great love, while pointing out that Earth must work out its own 'destiny' without interference. Since then, hundreds of meetings have been recorded, indicating a large number of extra-terrestrial races on or above the Earth who, without direct interference, are choosing to play a significant role in our evolution.

Whether from the Book of Revelation in the Bible, old memories of Atlantis, prophecies from both ancient and current times, spiritual guidance, extra-terrestrial intelligence or scientists and biologists – the message is the same: a Time of Awakening is upon us.

Newspapers are also getting into the act with headlines such as: *Is it Armageddon and the Apocalypse or the Advent of New Consciousness? Is Jesus going to descend in a cloud to judge the living and the dead or will we be rescued by extra-terrestrials?* Recently, even before the *Evening Standard* newspaper ran a small article that said, *If, by the time you read this, earthquakes have devastated London, fire has destroyed Buckingham Palace and the Thames has started lapping around your ankles, do not be surprised*, an American magazine said:

The Time has come. You are chosen to lift your eyes from darkness to light. You are blessed to see a new day on Planet Earth. Because your hearts have yearned to see Peace where war has reigned, to show mercy where cruelty has dominated and to know love where fear has frozen hearts, you are privileged to usher real healing into the world.'

No matter where we look or turn, we cannot escape the message to WAKE UP.

Part Two

WAYS TOWARDS
INNER GUIDANCE

6

THE HEALING POWER OF THOUGHT

Once awake, what do we do?

First we must recognise that we have cut ourselves off from God and nature, separated intellect from emotion, internal from external, mind from body and body from spirit. We are dismembered like a Shaman or medicine man who, when undergoing his training, suffers a rending apart of everything that constituted his physical, mental, emotional and spiritual reality. Unless he can heal himself, through a reintegration of all his parts, the Shaman fails his initiation. We, like the Shaman, are moving through an initiation in which, to heal ourselves, we must re-member, or reconnect to, all that we have been separated from. Unless we do this we remain powerless to help ourselves, each other or the world.

I am reminded of a children's story I saw on television in which a teacher, desperate to occupy the attention of a recalcitrant student, tore to shreds a map of the world. Thinking it an impossible task he gave it to the student to put together. Within a few minutes the boy was back, the task completed. Astounded, the teacher asked how he did it. The boy replied, 'I looked at the pieces of torn-up world and turned them over. On the other side I found a torn-up man. When I put the man together, the world came together and was whole again.'

Change from within

When we are awake enough to recognise that to heal the planet we must first heal ourselves, the next step is to explore how to go about it. There are literally hundreds of techniques we can use to put ourselves together. In fact, this generation is replete with self-improvement courses. There are courses on how to love yourself, how to know yourself, how to love others, how to deal with emotions such as anger, fear and jealousy, how to communicate, how to develop ESP. The list is almost endless. However, many of them work along lines of behaviour modification, structuring new ways of how to act and not necessarily how to be. In other words, they work from the outside in and not from the inside out, but we cannot change the outside without first changing the inside.

As a schoolgirl at a Roman Catholic convent, I said prayers morning, noon and night, as well as before and after each lesson. I repeated the same words in German, Spanish, French or Latin, on my knees or standing, depending on the whim of the teacher. Before hockey, tennis and gym we genuflected in front of horrendous statues of Jesus bleeding on the Cross. Prayers were an incomprehensible, meaningless gobbledegook of jumbled words.

I had absolutely no idea of the power of prayer until, years later, I took things into my own hands. I prayed about plants and animals and discovered a response. I prayed over food I cooked, for both myself and others, and found that despite my inexperience and their own digestive problems, no one suffered. I silently prayed about people I saw on trains, buses or planes who looked lonely or depressed and was often rewarded by an unexpected smile.

My most meaningful prayers were, and still are, the ones I make up as I go along. A story about Mohammed describes his journey along a wild and winding road, when he discovers a beggar on his knees, praying in the dust. Mohammed stops and asks the beggar what he's doing. When the beggar replies that he is saying his prayers, Mohammed is outraged. 'Prayers must not be said like this . . . you must follow the correct ritual . . . say the right formula ... have a sense of reverence ...' The beggar pleads with Mohammed to teach him the best way to pray and Mohammed does so.

Further along the road, Mohammed hears the voice of God booming out of the rocks. 'How could you do this to one of my children who prayed to me from his heart? Now all he does is recite a meaningless ritual from his head.'

St Germain supposedly said: 'Thoughts can never become things until they are clothed with feeling.' Prayers are the same. Without feeling, they are meaningless.

For Christians, the Lord's Prayer is the most commonly used prayer. Paul Solomon's interpretation of this prayer gave new meaning to the words for me:

'*Our Father*' (I address this request to the origin of myself – physically, mentally, spiritually and emotionally),

'*which art in Heaven*' (the point inside me, a quiet and beautiful place where God, or the highest in me, dwells),

'*hallowed be Thy Name*' (describes what I feel to be the good, or God part of me that strives for my highest good).

'*Thy Kingdom come*' (I ask the highest in me to direct my life),

'*Thy Will be done*' (let my higher God self make decisions for me instead of my lower personality self),

'*in earth as in heaven*' (until my daily life and activities reflect the same peace as the Kingdom of heaven within me).

'*Give us our daily bread*' (does not mean feed the starving in Ethiopia, or elsewhere, but rather feed *all* my bodies, stimulate my mind, calm my emotions, balance and heal my physical body).

'*Forgive us as we forgive*' (help me to recognise and release any situations that cause barriers between myself and others).

'*Lead me not into temptation*' (give me the strength or power to be strong in the face of temptation).

'*Thine is the Kingdom*' (acknowledges that there is a higher power and authority – I will credit that and not just pretend it came from me personally, that is my ego).

'*The power and the glory*' (a continuation of this recognition of a higher power and a blessing and thank God for it).

'*Amen*' signifies 'I have commanded it so. I expect this will be done.' Kings of old used to stamp letters and messages with these words. There was not a single doubt that their command would be carried out. When we pray, we should have the same expectation in order for our prayers to be effective. Instead, and again in Paul's words, 'most of us pray to a God who can't hear very well for something we believe we do not deserve.'

My favourite prayer is the one I learned in Bulgaria: a prayer taught by Beinsa Douna:

The disciple must have a heart as pure as a crystal,
A mind as bright as the sun,
A soul as vast as the Universe
and a spirit as powerful as God
and one with God. Amen.

Amongst many prayers Beinsa Douna also taught this prayer for healing:

Lord Thou art the source of all life; send me Thy
regenerating strength to treat my mind, my heart, my
spirit and my soul. Heal me from all suffering, from all
physical and psychic illness, and grant me health, strength,
life, youthfulness and beauty. Help me to develop the gifts
and talents within me so that I may live, learn and serve
Thee better. Amen.

Prayer is a prescription for healing. During a ten-month study of patients admitted to the coronary care unit of San Francisco General Hospital, 192 patients were prayed for by home prayer groups; 201 patients were not prayed for. Neither patients, nurses nor doctors knew which patients were in what group. Each patient had five to seven people praying for him/her, twenty-four hours a day.

The prayed-for patients required virtually no antibiotics, no endotracheal intubation (a tube inserted into the throat and attached to a ventilator) and did not develop pulmonary oedema (lungs filling with fluid because of heart problems). The non-prayed for patients developed many of these symptoms.

An organisation called Spindthrift spent years researching the effectiveness of prayer. They tested the interaction between prayer and seeds and found the ones that were prayed over were thicker, higher and healthier. They also prayed over seeds they deliberately made unhealthy with salt. The results were even more striking. Prayer worked better when seeds were under stress. They also found that doing everything they could but letting go of the result – i.e. 'Thy will be done' – was more effective than trying to affirm 'my will be done'.

Prayers said aloud on our knees have a different effect than prayers said silently in our heads. Rather like writing a dream down, to *speak* a prayer aloud makes visible what is invisible and helps our hearts to open.

To bless or pray over food restores some of the life-force lost through cooking or lack of freshness. At a big luncheon in South Africa, a priest invited by our hostess to say grace, simply raised his eyes skyward and said, 'Ta, Pa.' I often say this myself now.

Although not exactly a 'proper' prayer, if I am not sure what to do in a particular situation I simply say (in my head) 'If it's in my best or highest interests, increase the desire in me to do this or go there. If not, decrease the desire in me.' If I have a major question, I write the words down and put the paper under my pillow overnight. I always wake up knowing and feeling what to do. I also sometimes say to myself: if I was pure love, or pure truth, or my higher or God self, without personality or ego, what would I do? Or say? Something in me appears to respond and enables me to behave in a different manner.

Meditation

Change from within demands getting in touch within, as most psychologists, therapists and religious instructors would agree. To live in harmony with the world around us we must live in harmony with our inner selves. Meditation is the key. If prayers are a way to talk to God, meditation is to listen to the answer.

In Chapter 2 I said that meditation transformed my life. Before this, I was an accident-prone, self-conscious, apologising-for-virtually-every-breath-I-took victim. Initially, to learn how to meditate was, for me, very difficult. I read that it was imperative that I sit cross-legged, close my eyes and blank my mind. I did and not only got cramp but itched and twitched in places I never knew were there before.

My mind refused to go blank, and raced from thoughts of what I would eat for breakfast, lunch and supper to all the things I had left undone the previous week. I bought more books. One said contemplate, another said concentrate; some said close your eyes, while others said keep them open, stare at a blank wall, a candle, a flower, a pencil. I tried them all. In the beginning I got up at 6.30 a.m.; when this did not work I got up at 6 a.m., then 5 then 4 a.m., until I was spending three hours a day, before going to work, furiously trying to still my mind, concentrate, contemplate, while agonising pains racked my stiff and resistant body.

Finally, in desperation, wondering how on earth anyone could find inner peace through such torture, I decided to abandon all the techniques I had read about. I still got up at 4 a.m. but I stretched my legs out and leaned with my back against a wall. I breathed in to the count of four, held my breath to the count of four, and sighed the breath out to the count of four. This gave my mind something to do, although it often went off at a tangent. However, I persevered until I suddenly realised I was beginning to sleep better and, although what I did was not meditation, through conscious breathing my body began to relax and co-operate with me, rather than fight against me.

Having established a rhythm of breathing, which became more or less automatic, I decided to focus on the top of my head, my forehead, eyes and so on, down through my body to my toes. Initially I could never get from my head to my toes without some distraction but I always went back to the beginning and started again. Gradually I began to control my mind and I found that by the time I reached my toes, my body was so relaxed it was almost as if it wasn't there. I then practised moving my awareness from my toes to the top of my head and found myself arriving in a space where my mind truly did seem to be blank, empty and open.

I felt incredible peace and love, a sense of merging with something far beyond my normal physical consciousness. My life began to change. I saw the events and circumstances of my life in a different way. Living from the inside out rather than the outside in enabled me to deal with my work, family, friends and problems without stress or undue emotional reaction.

Over the years, meditation became the foundation from which I moved into the day. It was as necessary as food and put me in touch with a source of guidance, healing and help which completely changed my life. Much later, I discovered there are as many different ways to meditate as there are flowers in a garden. Also that I could have found a class in which to learn which would no doubt have been far less painful and time-consuming. However, I did learn for myself that there should not be any rigid rules.

The books I read at the beginning were written in such a way that to even think of not crossing your legs in a yoga-like position was almost a sin. I now believe that, although there are many simple guidelines which can be helpful, it is far more important to discover what works best for you and this requires experimentation. Meditation should also bring a dynamic energy into our lives which enables us to improve the quality of life – it should not be an escape or an opting out but rather an opting in.

Meditation is a conversation not only with our inner selves but also with the God in us, the highest in us. If you or I decide to have a chat and we have children around, it is more than likely they will interrupt with, 'Mummy, Sally smacked me', 'Mummy, I want a drink of water.' If we had taken the trouble to occupy the children first, given them a glass of water and crayons or toys to play with, they would probably leave us in peace. When we try to meditate or go within, our minds and bodies behave exactly like two spoiled children who demand attention from us and, in various ways, distract us.

If we take care of them first they will tend to co-operate with us rather than resist. For the body this means taking a few minutes to stretch, breathe, tense, tighten and then relax the muscles; to occupy the mind, use imagination to fill the body with light or colour, then visualise a garden, a meadow, a beach, a mountain, a lake or stream – or the colours of the rainbow. It does not matter whether this comes from the memory of an actual place, a picture or an image you make up as you go along. It does need to be a place that engenders feelings of joy and delight.

Also the more you can let your imagination play, the better. For example, if you imagine a garden, think of the breeze rustling the leaves of the trees, the sound of birds, or water trickling, bubbling, feel the sun on your face, the grass under your feet, smell the flowers, hug a tree, splash water on your face. The more you can stimulate your inner senses to come alive, the less distracted you will be by your outside environment.

You also begin to create a safe space, as well as a backdrop – rather like a stage set – against which your inner life can unfold. To take the trouble to do these things before any deep inner work or meditation will help whatever you do afterwards to work better. They are a preparation for meditation but not meditation itself.

Some people find it easier to play music in the background but I suggest that if you are a beginner you do not use music all the time because it fixes in your subconscious the idea, 'I can only do this with music.' Then, in the future, if you are sitting for hours on a plane, train or bus, or are away from home, your meditation may not work. From my own experience I also suggest that it is better to start with a minute or two of sitting quietly, and gradually extend it as the days go by, rather than force an hour which may be difficult.

A very simple attunement to one's inner self is to sit for a moment or two, eyes closed, and say: 'I am in communion with the essence of my being.' The two words – 'communion' and 'essence', have an effect on our consciousness similar to that of saying: 'Be still and know that I am God.' It commands instant respect. Every cell in the body responds. As you say it, breathe deeply. This exercise will strengthen you and lead you into deeper and more prolonged moments of stillness.

For me, meditation works best early in the morning or last thing at night – preferably both! I feel more comfortable taking time out to sit or kneel, although I also sometimes meditate in bed. However, many of my friends feel they are in a meditative state while working in the garden, washing dishes, painting a picture, listening to a favourite piece of music, watching a rising or setting sun or gazing at a beautiful view. And this may be so for you.

Ultimately everything we do should become a living meditation. If we can, at least once a day, by what ever means are available, take the time to become still, receptive, and align with our spiritual selves, we will find we are no longer at the mercy of outside circumstances. We will develop our inner strength, need less sleep, improve our health and the quality of life generally.

Western culture emphasises the use of left brain logic. Two and two makes four and anything I cannot see, feel, hear, taste and touch does not exist. We deny the value of the right brain's ability to imagine, intuit, listen, sense and feel. To take time deliberately to drop the chatter and logic of the left brain and move into the rich creativity of the right through meditation restores balance and harmony.

In the final chapter of this book I include a few examples of ways in which to use visualisation as a preparation for meditation as well as some visualisation exercises which, rather like dreams, can help us explore different facets of ourselves as well as our past, present and future. Remember that as long as these parts remain hidden and buried they have power over us. When we discover them, and let them speak to us and heal and help them they, too, like body and mind, begin to co-operate with us rather than unconsciously holding us back.

The power of thought

Another step in putting ourselves together is to understand the power of thought. Thought is the glue that holds the universe together – thoughts, which are made up from the beliefs we have about ourselves and life, create the reality in which we live. I learned this lesson in the following way. For years my family disapproved of what I did and thought I was mad to drop a regular job and salary in order to wander about the world doing the sort of work I do today. Each time I went home, for days beforehand I would imagine who was going to say what, and wish I did not feel obliged to put in an occasional appearance.

Every time exactly what I thought would happen did happen – often leaving me enraged and upset. After many similar visits I suddenly realised I was creating what happened so the next time, before I went, I imagined saying to my mother, 'I know you do not understand what I do but instead of attacking me why don't you simply say, "I don't understand what you do but good luck anyway."'

I then imagined light washing through both of us. For the first time there was no criticism or questioning, she simply accepted me. It taught me how the power of our thoughts affects what happens to us as well as the value of inner communication.

Energy follows thought, so if I constantly worry about war, starvation and poverty – or even my son falling off a motorbike – I am actually increasing the likelihood of their happening. If I think I have an ugly body and hate myself, chances are my body, which is highly responsive to mind-power, will reflect that. By contrast, if I think beautiful, loving and appreciative thoughts about my body as the vehicle for my experience on this planet, it is likely to be beautiful and healthy.

During the course of my practice as a healer I have been involved with lots of experiments in which we took a random selection of people off the street and put them in a room with a highly competent healer. We then wired both the healer and the patients to a brain scan monitor. Initially everyone's pattern was different. When the healer put her hands on the shoulders of each person and thought of them, that person's brain wave rhythm became identical to that of the healer. It happened without exception, to everyone in the room.

We then took another group, again picked at random off the street. This time we placed them individually in various houses and apartments in and around London. We again monitored their brain wave rhythms with that of the healer, who remained where she was. One by one, she was given the Christian names of the participants in the experiments and again in each case, as she thought of that person, their brainwave became identical with hers. Her energy following her thoughts caused something to happen.

In other experiments we used muscle-testing or kinesiology. We sat someone in front of a group, muscle-tested them as they were, sent them out of the room, and told the group to send either good or nasty thoughts (collectively good or collectively nasty). In every case, when the person came back into the room and was tested again, the 'good' thoughts, such as 'you are wonderful', strengthened the muscles, while 'bad' thoughts – 'you are horrible' – weakened them. (We always put them right later.)

The interesting thing here was that muscle-testing those sending out the bad thoughts showed they weakened themselves as well. I often use this test to illustrate to people who are full of self-pity what they are doing to their bodies. They often make immediate decisions to change.

Another type of experiment has involved groups of people flooding different cities with positive energy, love and healing, while monitoring the results with the aid of police and social services. In every case, there was a marked drop in burglaries, accidents and violence. If we want to help the planet we need to use our minds to send out thoughts of love, peace, abundance and health to everyone. This includes leaders, heads of state, kings, queens and presidents whose track record we may not approve.

If we can say 'the Divine in me acknowledges the Divine in you even if I do not like everything you do', we separate what someone does from who they are and can still act as catalysts for healing. Instead of demonstrating on the streets against nuclear bombs or starvation we need to bring peace into our own lives and families and try not to waste food. Do not feed energy into what is negative; starve it of its power and the world will be transformed. As Margaret Mead said: 'Never doubt that a small group of thoughtful, committed citizens can change the world; indeed, it is the only thing that ever does.'

Controlling our thoughts

Many of us believe we cannot control or change our thoughts. 'This is just the way I am, the result of how I was brought up and what has happened in my life.' A thought is only a belief about something. If we can change our beliefs we can change our thoughts and move beyond limiting behaviour patterns.

A tiny example might be that I have a next-door neighbour whom I avoid because I believe he is arrogant and difficult. Years later something happens that forces us to communicate. I suddenly realise he is not arrogant but shy and preoccupied with work. I change my belief about him.

Even people who believe they cannot change surely do not think in the same way at seventy-seven as they did at seventeen? Life experiences change us all, and at this time world events are pushing us to move almost beyond belief of any kind. This means we are free to respond, in the moment, to whatever comes into our lives – which is the true meaning of the word responsibility.

For example, if I am convinced that only homeopathy works and I deny the value of allopathic medicine, it is quite probable that at some point in my life I am going to need penicillin. If I refuse the benefits of penicillin I may prolong my illness – I am limiting myself. If, on the other hand, I am open to the idea that, although I prefer homeopathy and alternative medicine, I may at some time need a blood transfusion, operation or some other form of medical treatment, it frees me up. To live beyond belief simply means acknowledging that what works for us one day is not necessarily going to be the same tomorrow or next week. It means being flexible, adaptable and willing to change instantly.

Beliefs are all right as long as they provide a loose supportive structure, but when they become inflexible, judgemental and restrictive, it is time to drop them. If your life is full of tension, fear and unhappiness, look at what you are thinking. Peace Pilgrim, an extraordinary woman who inspired many people to work for peace from 1953 to 1981 and who walked thousands of miles across the United States preaching global understanding and the need for peace, said: 'The criterion by which you can judge whether the thoughts you are thinking and the things you are doing are right for you is – have they brought you inner peace?'

Remember, your mind and your attitudes are two things that

you have absolute control over. Also remember that you can only think one thought at a time, so replace a negative thought with the memory of something that makes you happy. It does not matter what it is – your favourite food or television programme – simply switch into another mode.

Beliefs affect our emotional responses. We think they happen to us as the result of another person's actions or attitude. In fact, we can choose whether to react or not, providing we involve the power of our mind.

Most emotional reactions are the direct result of the beliefs we have about ourselves. For example I, feeling insecure, go to a party and my husband dances a little too long, for my liking, with another woman. I am jealous. I have various options. I can interrupt, make a scene or say I want to go home. I can dance with someone else, I can go to the bathroom and cry, or take the car and leave.

If I act while stewing with suppressed emotion I am (a) going to regret it and (b) will probably make a fool of myself. Whatever I do is an attempt to get his attention and reassurance. Through emotional reaction that does not examine the underlying cause or belief, in order to get love I make myself thoroughly disagreeable and unlovable. It is completely irrational. If I could recognise that, in this moment, I am feeling vulnerable because of my own lack of self-worth – and be honest with myself about it, without blaming my husband – 'you're doing this to me'; if I could accept responsibility, look at the underlying cause, which is the belief that I am less interesting and attractive than my husband's dancing partner, maybe I could handle it in a different way. Maybe I could, with a smile on my face, tap him on the shoulder and gently say, 'My turn now.'

No matter how much we think emotions happen to us there is a moment of decision, an opportunity to choose between one reaction and another. The reaction we usually subconsciously choose is the one that gets the most results from the person or situation we believe hurt us. Most negative emotions come from lack of belief in ourselves. If I feel good about who I am, the fact that my husband dances too long with someone else will probably amuse me. I am not dependent on his attention for how I feel about myself. I do not give my power away to outside influences or let them affect what I feel, do or say. Even if I do feel emotionally vulnerable, by engaging my mind I can change what was previously an automatic reflex response.

Confused beliefs affect all of us. Recently a friend told me how, at a time of great personal crisis, he went to see a counsellor to pour out his problems.

'As I spoke,' he said, 'her eyes became a little glazed, she made strange grimaces which she tried to hide by propping her face on her hands. I thought she was so bored by my revelations that she was trying to stop herself yawning. In my family, no one ever listened to me and I became angry that even when I paid someone to listen they still switched off. I decided to leave. As I pushed my chair back, the door opened and a woman popped her head into the room saying, "Nancy, I know you've just been to the dentist to have a tooth out and I wanted to check that you were OK."

'I suddenly realised that she was in agony and that I was projecting on to her all my childhood experience. If this other woman had not opened the door at that moment, I would probably never have gone to another counsellor again and simply carried on with the belief, "No one ever listens to me." It shocked me into recognising that I had draped this belief over anyone I had any deep personal contact with, which created a barrier that made it come true.'

Most of us project our beliefs on to everyone around us – especially our families. A mother came to see me concerned that her son, aged eight, would only eat Coco-Pops. I said, 'Does it matter?' She was outraged and told me that children should eat healthy food – plenty of fruit, vegetables, meat, fish and eggs. I asked why. As if I was a moron, she spent the next two hours explaining why. I finally pointed out that her belief about what a good mother was – to feed a child a healthy diet – was so fixed she was unable to respond to why the child was behaving like this.

Her need was to be seen as a 'good mother' which made her oblivious to the child's needs. It was a power struggle and probably the only way he could assert himself or get her attention. She finally saw that good mothering was not merely dependent on the quality of food a child ate, and followed my suggestion to start eating Coco-Pops herself. After about ten days of them both eating Coco-Pops for every meal, the child got bored and began to eat normally. The mother realised that quality time together, companionship and fun, rather than the rigidity of unconscious rules coming out of duty and responsibility, transformed both her and her son's life.

Setting up expectations

If we expect ourselves, our children, or anyone else, to behave in a certain way, we and they will. An illustration of this is an experiment conducted in 1966 to study the expectations of the experimenters. Scientists ran rats through a maze. Half the rats had portions of their brains surgically removed, the remaining half received identical incisions, but no brain tissue was removed. The experimenters were told that the purpose was to learn the effects of brain lesions on learning. Some of the scientists were told they had brain-damaged rats, but in fact did not. Others were told they had intact rats, but actually had brain-damaged ones.

The results were amazing. The rats which were thought by scientists to be brain-damaged, but were really totally intact, did not perform as well as rats thought to be normal. The brain-damaged rats who were thought by the scientists to be normal performed better than the rats who were actually normal but *thought* to be brain-damaged.

It was clear from this study that the scientists' expectations influenced the outcome of the experiments. These tests are very similar to the ones I described earlier using kinesiology to determine the effect of our thoughts on another person.

Thoughts change perceptions

Another more recent experiment showed that our thinking affects not only what we see, but also *changes* what we see. In a quantum physics experiment, scientists disagreed over what matter was made of. Some said particles, some said waves of light. When experiments were conducted to find the correct answer, it was discovered that those who believed in particles saw particles and those who believed in waves saw waves.

Was there a right or wrong answer? No. Reality depends entirely on our point of view. They also saw that they could affect the movement of both the waves and the particles through the projection of their thoughts.

This is similar to the experiments Marcel Vogel made with liquid crystals. When he projected the thought of a particular shape into the liquid, it solidified into the shape of his thought.

Remote viewing or thought projection

Seminars that teach thought projection, or remote viewing, are now even more popular than those that teach astral-travel or past-life (regression) therapy. Remote viewing is another term for a telepathic, clairvoyant sensing of what is happening so far away that it cannot be seen by the physical eye.

'Remote viewing' was a phrase coined by the American psychic Ingo Swann, who used it to describe the psychic viewing of distant locations. George Bush used 'remote viewers' to search for Scud missiles during the 1991 Gulf War. Remote viewing, when used by Air, Army or Navy intelligence, is a form of psychic spying.

Before using our own minds for remote viewing we must understand that artificial, electro-magnetic energy can create around us a kind of mental pollution, like a fog that disrupts brainwave patterns. This means that television and radio towers, electric wires that criss-cross the country, radiation from household appliances such as microwaves, TVs, radios and computers, disturb our emotional and mental clarity. Research shows that disruptive electro-magnetic fields are far higher in areas where the percentage of suicide, murder, depression and fatal accidents are also high.

The good news is that there are now a variety of instruments and machines on the market that counteract mental smog and re-synchronise both left and right brainwave rhythms. One is the Binaural Signal Generator, developed by Robert Monroe, which stimualtes the mind while relaxing the body. Another is the 'Teslar' invented by Andre Puararich. The Teslar is a tiny instrument built into a watch which, when worn, neutralises electronic pollution.

Mind projection techniques have been used for eons. Buddhist Lamas in Tibet, Egyptian priests and priestesses, magicians and metaphysicians knew how to create thought forms and project them to far distant places. The Old Testament describes how Elija (Elisha) used psychic power to save Israel from military defeat while Joan of Arc did the same for France in battles against the English.

To develop the skills of mind projection or remote viewing, which is really a form of telepathy, we must first empty our heads of the logical thoughts that say it's impossible. Then imagine being a tree, a flower, a blade of grass – even a chair, a knife, fork or spoon. Practise, practise, and practise again. With closed eyes, imagine colours and favourite scenes and places – in your mind's eye, literally *be* there. Imagine lifting your etheric or astral body out of your physical one. Move it left, right and above your head. Loosen your attachment to the physical reality via your imagination. *Pretend* (*pre* meaning before I *tend* to think this, or do that). The key to successful telepathic or remote vewing is to empty the mind, listen and allow whatever thoughts or ideas surface, without judging them as right or wrong.

Mind projection, when used in Gestalt-type family sculpture, allows us first to intuitively sense and second to understand the thoughts and feelings of the people we grew up with.

Of course this exercise can be used for any other relationship issue. Mind projection enables us to literally 'walk in another man's shoes' – which is especially useful when dealing with so-called enemies.

Psychometry – the art of holding an object in one's hand and intuitively picking up information, either connected to it or about its owner – can also help us develop the ability to remote view.

As it says in Romans (12.2): 'Be ye not conformed to the world but be ye transformed by the renewing of your mind.'

The power to heal

The power of the mind to heal the body or change it is limitless. Most of us are familiar with stories such as that of Admiral Shattock who avoided a hip replacement operation by re-growing his hip bone. He did this through meditation, visualisation (of healthy bone and bone-marrow, pictures of which he studied in medical books from his local library) and by directing his mind to heal his body. Admiral Shattock's doctors told him this was impossible and an utter waste of time and energy. The Admiral made medical history and his case was written up in the *Lancet*. He later went on to cure a prostate problem in the same way.

Ian Gawler, a doctor from Australia, was told by his doctors after months of chemotherapy and a leg amputation to put all his affairs in order. They believed he had no more than two days to live. Dr Gawler refused to accept the diagnosis. He decided to use his mind and imagination, combined with a variety of alternative medicines, to get better. He did – and now runs a clinic in Melbourne designed to help other cancer patients fight back as he did.

Joan Borysenko, author of *The Power of the Mind to Heal*, says: 'As a former cancer cell biologist, with a doctorate in Medical Science from Harvard Medical School, I know a lot about the pathways through which the body gets sick and how it recovers. I also know that there is no such thing as an incurable illness.'

Dr Deepak Chopra, who describes his approach to health and medicine as quantum healing, says, 'Science declared that we are physical machines that have somehow learned to think. Now it dawns that we are thoughts that have learned to create a physical machine.'

A fascinating example of the mind–body connection is the reaction of many people to placebos, when these are admin-istered, in conjunction with new experimental drugs, in clinical trials. In one such test a group of cancer patients was given chemotherapy while another group received placebos. Three-quarters of the placebo group lost their hair because they expected chemotherapy to cause this. Even rats given immuno-suppressive drugs in apple juice would later immunosuppress just from the taste of apple juice.

Placebos to control depression, headaches and even pain, have proved to be nearly as effective as real medicine. One story describes how a man awoke in the night with an acute migraine headache. Fumbling for aspirin in the dark, he swallowed three tablets, lay quietly until the pain receded and eventually fell asleep. In the morning he found he had swallowed 3 buttons his wife had left on the bedside table.

Mental stress can affect our immune system to the point that we get colds, 'flu and even pneumonia. Exams, deadlines, competitions, anything that pushes us to perform when we may, consciously or unconsciously, feel inadequate can damage our health. Lack of forgiveness, holding onto thoughts of resentment or 'if only' can cause arthritis, depression and heart attacks. Emotional imbalance destroys physical balance. Many doctors describe fear as a bigger killer than cancer or Aids.

Thoughts are creative. If we think money is bad we will draw to us financial problems based on lack of it. If we think the world is a bad place, we draw to us bad situations. We must learn to think creatively, causally, rather than reactively. We must also learn to think about what we think.

Many philosophers say 'To change your life, change your thinking.' Miraculous recovery from illness and accident show how true this is. Thought creates experience. Whatever now presents itself in life is the result of our own creativity. If it is not enjoyable, instead of condeming it bless, release and change it.

If we think life is falling apart, we must think again. Think a new thought. Make a new choice. To do this we must become very clear about what we want to do, be and have. As Dyani Ywahoo says: 'That fire of clear mind is in everyone and to remove any obscuration of its clarity is the duty of all people in this time . . .'

To change an experience in the moment we need to act quickly, on the spur of an instant thought combined with instinctive gut feeling, rather than let our slow, reflective minds kill the idea. If we want to change a root thought we must act in accordance with the new idea quickly. We must not let negative self-talk get in the way.

If an inner, nagging, critical voice holds you back, the following suggestions may help to overcome it:

1 Draw it and mentally dialogue with it.

2 Imagine your inner critic is sitting opposite you and question him/her as to the why and wherefore of the criticism.

3 Mentally question the critic or even write the questions on paper. For example: '*Why* will I forget my speech in front of the Queen, or my local Girl Guide group? *Why* do you think I've chosen the wrong clothes for . . . my first dinner, dance or date . . . job interview . . . wedding . . . funeral . . . my son's graduation? *Why* am I not capable of flying alone to Timbuctoo? Or cooking supper for 30 people?' Listen to the answers that will pop into your mind spontaneously. Some of them may sound like this: 'Because . . . you have never done it before; you have a bad memory (everyone knows this) . . . you will make a fool of yourself . . . you are too fat, thin, tall, small . . . you never went to University . . . you have no sense of colour . . . etc.'

   Do not stop there. Ask: 'What makes you think I have no sense of colour, a bad memory, am afraid of doing what I've never done before?' Persevere until you discover and understand where this kind of negative thought and self-criticism came from.

Another method is auto-suggestion or self-hypnotism, which can be done by listening to a tape, even while asleep. Napoleon Hill, who wrote many self-help books, spent hours whispering words of encouragement into the ears of his sleeping, handicapped son. Hill constantly repeated affirmations of physical and mental health and well-being. His son responded and became far more active and happy.

Pre-sleep, as well as sleep suggestion, is a wonderful way to alter negative mind-sets, and can also rejuvenate and heal the body. Jo, a South African friend who had breast cancer, and then a double mastectomy, puts her recovery down to nightly doses of Louise Hay tapes. Jo never even consciously listened to more than ten minutes of each tape because she fell asleep. Every morning she awoke bright, cheerful and healthy. And today, she no longer suffers from cancer.

In addition to accelerated learning techniques, which stimulate mindpower and memory, now we even have machines to boost IQ and mental agility. Even without brain-stimulating, thought-provoking instruments, we still have the power of our minds to change our lives. In the words of G. K. Chesterton: 'Real development is not leaving things behind, as on a road, but drawing life from them, as from a root.' Let's use the power of thought and imagination to do just that.

The power to re-create ourselves

Physics, metaphysics, science and technology now agree that everything is subjective, interrelated and determined by how we choose to look at anything. In other words, science reinforces the metaphysical teachings that say we truly do create our own reality and that there is no such thing as inanimate matter. Everything, from a cloud to a tree to a rock to the chairs we sit on or the car we drive, is infinitely responsive to our thoughts. We are creators of our own universe, we *can* cause things to happen.

This means we must take responsibility for our thinking – move from judgement, which condemns, to discernment which is clear-seeing. We must open our hearts to life and recognise that we have the power to re-create ourselves, our lives, and, like the story at the beginning of this chapter, the world around us. We are literally child gods growing up to be what our Father is.

7

USING CRYSTALS FOR BALANCE AND VITALITY

Thought and electricity

Quantum physics has turned our thinking upside down and drastically altered our perception of reality so that a new paradigm (for change) is emerging. We now know that whatever we do, think, feel or imagine, influences the world around us. We as observers are not separate from what we observe; by merely looking at, or experiencing it, we change it. We impregnate it with a part of our own consciousness, our own energy.

Thought produces an electrical charge. Highly emotional thoughts carry a greater electrical charge. The atmosphere around us is also electrically charged. Electricity is tenacious of equilibrium; because thought produces electricity, the force field in which cells, atoms and molecules are created is affected by thought, which means that the invisible structure of our surroundings carries a record, or the memory, of these thoughts.

This is why psychics can pick up or tune into events that have taken place in a room or a house. They 'read' what the owners or previous inhabitants have unconsciously written into the molecular structure of the place, space and furniture. Psychometrists who can describe the history of old jewellery, paintings and *objets d'art* do the same thing. They decipher or interpret the impression or indentation left by past owners.

Crystals

Quantum physics proves that matter is a whirling mass of movement – a dance of quarks, protons and neutrons, sometimes seen as dots, sometimes waves – which is responsive to many energies including human. For example, a plant will respond well to a crystal placed near it, just as it will flinch if a live shrimp is dropped into boiling water in another room.

Crystals themselves, which mainly consist of silicon dioxide and water, are of a high vibrational frequency which bring up to their own vibratory level everything within a certain radius. Crystals emit energy which expands when positive patterns of thought oscillate around them. In other words, if we believe in their power they work better than if we do not.

Crystals are very much part of the new or quantum age in which we now live. They consist of millions of individual structural units of atoms called unit cells which link together in a network or pattern called a lattice. The effect of heat and pressure on these atoms rearranges them, causing crystallisation.

Quartz crystals react when squeezed or pressed. They produce a current of electricity called piezoelectricity, an oscillation, which is why crystals are used in clocks, watches, radios, television sets, computers and any other electronic device that demands high precision. If heat is applied to natural quartz the stability of the atomic structure is disturbed, causing the negative and positive energies at either end of the crystal to change. As the crystal attempts to regain stability, by re-arranging the atoms of its internal structure, it produces opposite charges at either pole, which is called pyroelectricity.

Marcel Vogel, a research scientist and one of the world's most renowned crystallographers, had such an affinity with crystals that he could produce a flame from a crystal just by stroking it with his fingers. The ancient Greeks used crystals to light the sacred flame of the Olympiad. Australian Aboriginals, New Guinea tribesmen and in fact most indigenous peoples, including the American Indians, consider crystals to be the brain cells of Mother Earth, star seeds left by the gods or other planets, which have the power to heal, guide and transmit information. Many of the Edgar Cayce readings suggested that to wear a crystal or stone would give strength, vitality and protection to the wearer.

Crystals and healing

For twenty-five years quartz crystals have played a vital role in my life. I used them, in conjunction with prayers, meditation, visualisation and affirmation, to heal myself after an accident in which my face and head were smashed. The results were so successful I began to include, and still do, crystal work in my healing practice.

Crystals are not a magic cure-all, not a substitute for orthodox medicine. They can help kick-start the body – a little like recharging a car battery – to balance itself to a point of optimum health and efficiency. Crystals are transformers of energy and balance everything with which they come in contact.

During many experiments with doctors, both allopathic and alternative, we found that crystals accelerated healing and reduced pain. This included broken bones, post-operative scarring and skin problems as well as emotional stress. During one experiment we took people, one by one, off the street and measured their electro-magnetic or auric field. We then gave them a glass of ordinary water to drink. Nothing happened. As soon as we gave them crystal-charged water – water in which a quartz crystal has soaked for a minimum of twenty minutes and preferably longer – this field expanded to fifteen feet around the body. The initial test was with 300 people and in every case the result was the same.

We may say, 'So what – who cares about the size of an aura – especially when to most people it is invisible.'

However, the aura, almost like a bubble that enfolds us, is our very own private and protective space. It is an electrical field made up of a number of subtle or invisible bodies which swirl and move, shrink when we feel depressed, expand when we are happy.

Illness, mental upset, emotional distress, drug and alcohol abuse, as well as accidents and non-resolved problems – from this and other lives – show up in these subtle bodies before they manifest as symptoms of disease in the physical body. In fact seeing auras can even help diagnose learning difficulties in young children.

It therefore makes good sense to clear the aura of imbalance – which shows up like a shadowy blob or discoloration – as an automatic part of both general healing and preventative medicine. Crystal energy breaks up and disperses disturbance in the subtle bodies, and helps to bring them into harmony and balance so that the auric field is cleared and recharged. This can be done by wearing a crystal, placing one on or near the body, drinking crystallised water or following some of the techniques I describe in my book *The Power of Gems and Crystals*.

Since writing this book hundreds of people have contacted me describing the results of their own crystal work. Sally, a woman in her late forties, was in hospital for tests before undergoing major surgery. After urine tests the doctors said to her, 'There must be some mistake. We will have to do it again. Your urine tested as pure as a mountain stream.'

Every day for seven days, to the increasing disbelief of both doctors and nurses, Sally produced urine as pure as a mountain stream. Initially embarrassed, she finally confessed to drinking crystallised water. Incidentally this works best if the crystal, which should be natural quartz and not man-made, lead crystal, is left in a glass, a jug or a bottle overnight. In fact the water can be topped up as it is used and the crystal left permanently in place.

Clifford Jones, also a crystal-water addict, was confronted on his doorstep by a man selling water purifiers. They proceeded to the kitchen, where Clifford watched the salesman's demonstration and saw that there was indeed greater clarity in the purified water than the water from the tap. He then remembered the water jug in which he kept a crystal and asked the salesman to compare this water with the machine purified water. To the salesman's amazement – and I think Clifford's too – the crystallised water tested, and tasted, better than the water purified through the machine.

Frances, who attended some of my crystal workshops, fell downstairs and hurt her back. She remembered hearing me speak about crystals being used to reduce pain and so, while waiting for the doctor, held her favourite crystal against her lower back. Within ten minutes she felt the pain ease. Since then she has used crystals many times on both herself and others. For Frances, crystals work best when placed on the area of pain and left for twenty to thirty minutes. (For best results, this should be done two to three times a day.)

Tom, a chain-smoker for fifty years, told me that he reluctantly accompanied his wife to a crystal shop and, while there, picked up a piece of amethyst, put it in his pocket and promptly forgot all about it. Two hours later he suddenly realised that since leaving the shop he had not smoked one cigarette, nor did he have any desire to do so. Wondering how this was possible he put his hand in his pocket and found the amethyst. Having previously mocked his wife for her interest in semi-precious gems he now decided that the amethyst calmed him to such an extent he no longer needed cigarettes. Overnight he stopped smoking. (He also went back to the shop to pay for the amethyst he had inadvertently taken and bought a number of other stones too!)

Jenny found that blue lace agate helped her sleep better while rose quartz held against her stomach after a miscarriage soothed feelings of distress and vulnerability. (Rose quartz is wonderful for any kind of love problem, including lack of self-love.) David, a doctor, put quartz clusters in his surgery and waiting-room and found his patients responded more quickly to his treatment than before.

Many healers use crystals, gems and minerals to balance and clear the chakras, the energy points in the body. Adolescents addicted to drugs and alcohol, when taught to see auras and treat them with crystal therapy, very quickly drop their addiction.

Jane and Harry, both vets, began to use crystals on animals and found that they too, like plants, food, humans and even machinery, responded well.

Among the many other ways crystals can help us is through counteracting LVF, or low frequency vibration, caused by fluorescent lighting, television, radio, microwave ovens and similar electrical equipment. LVF used to be a method of protecting food stored in warehouses from rats and mice, until it was discovered that it made the staff emotionally unstable and depressed.

Today our bodies are constantly bombarded with all sorts of stresses, from insecticide sprayed on our food and the synthetic fabrics we use, to the polluted atmosphere, noise and even one another. Crystal energy neutralises these stresses by altering their atomic, molecular structure, the atmosphere around them as well as our attitude to them. Crystals played a part in the technology that sent rockets to the moon. In the same way they expand and energise us, activate our abilities not only to cope but to reach for the stars. They clarify what we need to see and stimulate us to deal with the results, even when we do not want to.

Aside from improved health and a general sense of well-being, their effectiveness can be tested with kinesiology, biofeedback and Kirlian photography, a form of photograph invented by a Russian, Peter Kirlian, which registers the electro-magnetic field surrounding people, plants, animals and stones.

The power to heal is the power to control and move energy, whether it be from one part of the body to another or from one person to another person. Crystals amplify and transmit this energy. The principle is similar to using a microphone which brings the voice into sharp focus, amplifies and transmits it in a way not possible for the human voice on its own.

For complete healing on every level we need to remember that illness exists first in the non-physical realm of mind, feeling and even spirit. This means it is essential to examine the whole person, treat the cause and not just the symptom. Quantum healing is holistic healing in which crystals are an invaluable part because of their capacity to affect every level of matter or vibration as well as every aspect of a personality, whether mental, physical, emotional or spiritual.

Choosing crystals

Having shared many simple methods of crystal healing in my crystal book I do not want to duplicate them here. For those who are not familiar with crystal therapy I want to stress that the crystals I refer to are naturally grown, quartz and not man-made which, however pretty, do not have the same power to balance or transmit energy. Neither do polished or cut crystals have the same properties as those left uncut. It is as if their energy field is smoothed out and less active. However, for people who need to be calmed down, rather than stimulated, polished stones are beautiful to hold and relax with.

For bodywork I prefer larger crystals of approximately 6–8 inches (15–20 cms) in length. For personal use I like small crystals that are easy to stick inside a bra, purse or pocket.

I usually cleanse my crystals in sea water or sea-salt dissolved in water. I leave them for 36–70 hours and then dry them in the sun on silk, cotton or linen fabric. If they feel sticky from the salt, I polish them with natural fabric. There are dozens of methods for crystal cleansing. They can be held, point up, under fast-flowing tap water; bathed in a stream; smudged in the American Indian way with incense and herbs, or placed on an amethyst cluster for twenty-four hours. Some crystal owners prefer to bury them in the earth or leave them to bathe in the light of the sun or the moon. Others cover their crystals with brown rice or flower petals. In addition to sea water, my crystals love to be bathed in flower essences and aura-soma oils.

A simple rule of thumb when choosing gems and crystals is to remember that the more opaque or solid in colour and texture, the greater its ability to absorb trauma and induce peace. By contrast, the more clear and sparkling the gem, the more stimulating and energising its effect.

For example, *Herkimer diamonds* – tiny, double-terminated quartz crystals that look like diamonds and are only found in

Herkimer County, New York State – are wonderful to carry with us when we feel depressed. They sparkle and glow, give us an extra boost of energy and help to clear emotional blocks. Anyone affected by criticism and what they fear or imagine others think about them will benefit from clear quartz, which generates and activates energy and repels negativity.

By contrast Malachite, Lapis Lazuli, Sodalite, Jade, green Aventurine, Sugilite (sometimes called Luvalite) are all opaque stones which sooth, calm and balance. Although each gem has its own particular qualities they all help to bring us to a point of inner peace.

Green stones such as Malachite, Aventurine, Jade and Emerald are especially useful for balancing the heart chakra, particularly if we need to develop unconditional love and peaceful relationships with ourselves and others. Green is known as the fulcrum colour, meaning it is the midpoint between the 'hot' or earthy colours of red, orange and yellow, and the 'cool' colours of blue, indigo and violet. It is therefore a colour generally associated with healing, and can be used to balance any form of stress, whether physical, mental or emotional.

Sodalite, which is a deep, almost navy blue stone, and Sugilite, a pinky violet stone, are both excellent for increasing spiritual awareness and developing our third eye or inner vision. *Blue* stones such as Lapis Lazuli, Sapphire, Blue Lace Agate, Blue Calcite, Celestite, as well as Turquoise and Aquamarine which, though not an exact blue, belong to the blue family, are connected to the throat chakra and can help us to release any fear we may have to speak out and live our own truth without apology or explanation. In other words blue stones release constriction in the throat and help us to express our thoughts, feelings and creativity freely and without inhibition.

The stones that can most help us to face the challenges of the new millennium and overcome some of the symptoms I mentioned in Chapter 3 are, firstly, *quartz crystals*, because they awaken us to higher levels of awareness and shatter, or break open, fixed patterns of behaviour, crystallized thoughts and attitudes.

Smoky quartz, which can vary in colour from black to shades of grey, can help us deal with the effects of Pluto who pushes us into the underworld. Smoky quartz helps us to face everything we may have repressed or denied, consciously and unconsciously. It triggers us to find and heal our shadow and as we do this the smoky quartz often becomes clear.

Rutilated quartz, which is a crystal with tiny threads of silver or gold running through it, is sometimes known as the stone of communication; its threads resemble telephone wires that connect us to places and people anywhere in the world. Rutilated quartz helps to focus and direct the mind, and contains within it the power to link us to past and future, as well as to friends and family, no matter where they may be.

Watermelon Tourmaline, tri-coloured Fluorite and Sugalite (or Luvalite) are also very important stones for the last decade of this century. *Watermelon Tourmaline* – which is pink inside and dark green outside – illustrates two different energies or vibrations blended harmoniously together, one contained within the other, and yet unique and individual at the same time. Watermelon Tourmaline is the ideal gem for male/female relationships – not for parent/child or co-worker relationships. They stimulate empathy, communication and companionship, and generate feelings of support and understanding that are sometimes quite uncanny. Watermelon Tourmaline can also be used when someone is dying. The pink centre contained within the green symbolises the tunnel of death, and can bring a peaceful acceptance that the time has come to float through it.

Tri-coloured Fluorite, which combines purple, white and green, symbolises the blend of will, wisdom and love, as well as body, mind and spirit. It can be opaque or translucent and is very much a gem for the twenty-first century, as it helps us to bring down into material reality ideas of the spirit. It is also good for teeth and bones.

The conjunction of Uranus and Neptune in Capricorn is helping us to move beyond only trusting and using mainly left-brain logic, while we deny the value of right-brain intuition and imagination. *Sugilite* clears away the barriers between logic and intuition, stimulates creativity and helps us to make quantum leap mental shifts that open us to other dimensions. It can also, like a Record Keeper, a quartz crystal with a triangle engraved on one of its facets, activate our memory of other lives.

The first time I used Sugilite I was totally unaware of its almost magical properties. I held a tiny piece of it against my forehead. Every chakra responded and aligned itself with the others. It was as if an army sergeant had caught me slouching and told me to brace up. At the same time I felt as though my brain had been tied up with Sellotape which was now being ripped off. I remembered the Barbra Streisand film *On a Clear Day You Can See Forever* and felt a surge of excitement that, in that moment, I could do the same.

Later a disbelieving friend took the same piece of Sugalite to her car and lay back with it pressed firmly to her third eye, or centre of the forehead, brow chakra. She was literally zapped into the memory of another life which so shook her that she returned the stone to me in shaking hands. However, it also clarified why she was experiencing certain problems in her life at that time and enabled her to deal with them in a different way.

Pink Kunzite, just like Rose Quartz, can help us develop self-love, self-acceptance, and therefore unconditional love for others.

Self-healed crystals – crystals which, after removal from the earth, grow another point or layers of little triangles which form a glittering, translucent pattern as opposed to the rough break formed by the crystal broken from its source, are especially powerful for the new millenium. They have learned how to heal themselves, and can help us to do the same.

Some of the crystals I have had for ten years or more have recently mended themselves in a way that is for me miraculous. This is one of the reasons why I do not believe in clamping a crystal at one end with silver or gold in order to hang it on a chain. This stifles its growth and blocks its opportunity for change. Self-healed crystals can help us make the best of every event of our lives, no matter how devastating, and bring them to a point of completion and harmony.

Another gem for the future is the crystal known as the *Elestial*. Elestials align with angelic spheres and combine the elements of fire, water, earth and air. They are often smoky grey with a configuration of geometric patterns and double-terminated crystals contained within a cluster. They are very comfortable to hold in the hand, can activate the crown chakra, stabilise mental confusion and help us with our true essence or soul self.

When choosing crystals for the first time, trust your feeling and intuition rather than logic or what someone else thinks. An Aboriginal tribal elder told me once that when a crystal comes unexpectedly or spontaneously into our lives it is a gift from the universe, has grown itself especially for us and should be treated with extra care and respect. However, whether we buy, find or receive crystals as presents, they are all very special gifts from the universe. Do not, therefore, get over-anxious, fussed or confused when choosing one, the correct crystal for each of us will always turn up.

Experimenting with crystals

To discover how best they work, experiment. When I started using crystals I worked from intuition, trial and error. It was not until much later that I discovered scientific facts and explanations for what I sensed. Despite how much we learn about a crystal's geological make-up, and its ability to oscillate at different frequencies in clocks, watches, radios and computers, there is still a mystical X-factor that even scientists have not been able to decipher. An example of this is the way in which crystals will disappear and reappear, sometimes weeks later, in another room, even another house or country. We should not feel sad about this but rather love and release them, knowing that they have moved into another dimension, a higher frequency, in exactly the same way that we move into another dimension at the time of our death, or release from our physical body. Many of my own crystals have developed *rainbows*, which are brilliantly coloured when I am well and become pale when I am sick. Others have grown new, small crystals, almost like a plant sprouting buds.

Rainbows reflect the link between Heaven and Earth; they are a sign of angelic protection and love, a blessing from God. Often the colour prisms which form the rainbows in crystals are there as the result of a knock or a flaw. Because of this they help us to transform our own flaws and knocks into beauty and understanding. Rainbow crystals can help to bridge communication gaps and problems with others with humour, joy and laughter. They are an antidote to depression and taking life too seriously. If we feel disillusioned by life and carry a rainbow crystal in a purse or pocket we shall soon feel better.

One of my initial trial-and-error experiments was to sleep with crystals under my pillow. I found that sometimes this energy helped me to sleep, at other times it kept me awake so that I had to move them to the floor of another room. I also discovered that crystals stimulate both dreaming and the ability to remember dreams.

I found that if I listened to music with a crystal in my left hand the effect was far more profound. If I listened to a tape with a crystal in my right hand and put my left hand on the cassette, the sound affected my body in such a way that every cell seemed to vibrate to the music. I asked friends to experiment with music in this way themselves, both with and without crystals. They all reported the same results.

I wondered if crystals could amplify my sense of taste so, following an experiment described by Marcel Vogel, I put a few grains of pepper on a crystal. He said, 'Place your finger over the pepper on the crystal, close your eyes, visualise the pepper, then breathe the image into the crystal. Now wash both the crystal and your hands and breathe in the "pepper-energy" projected into the crystal.' I did this a number of times until my eyes watered and my throat felt peppery-sore. This experiment can be done with any vegetable or condiment and can actually improve our sense of taste.

To improve the quality of my meditation I held a crystal in both hands and breathed its energy into my heart. I breathed with a rhythm of inbreath and outbreath to the count of four. When I felt at one with the crystal I imagined light radiating between us and expanding around my body in such a way that it bathed everything and everybody around me. Sometimes I held my crystal point-up and on other occasions horizontally.

I found that to hold a crystal in my left hand enabled me to read and study better. I tried doing this both with and without crystals and I always seemed to remember information better with a crystal in my hand.

I also used crystals, like a telephone, to contact angels, guardians and guides. I imagined being inside the crystal, one with what I feel is the Divine Light of the mineral kingdom. With practice, I felt the atmosphere around me, as well as the energy within me, change. I began to ask questions, get answers and write them down. Initially I was afraid that I was making it up but the information became very clear and, in various ways, proved to be true.

Marcel Vogel's following tip on self-healing with a crystal is both simple and dynamic. In his words:

> To release unwanted tension in your body, hold the opposing tips of a crystal with your thumbs and forefingers. Draw your breath in, look at a face of the crystal, visualise the area in your body having discomfort, create the image of your body being well and free of pain, and pulse your breath.
>
> Draw your breath in again and pick another crystal face and repeat the above exercise. Now reverse the tips of the crystal to point in the opposite direction and repeat the same operation. Do this morning and night and most simple pains will be eliminated. If not see your doctor.

The re-emergence of crystals

Many years ago during a ceremony of dedication in which a giant crystal played a major part, those of us present were told that we had all been involved in the misuse of crystal power in the past. As a result the energy and power were withdrawn. Now, hundreds of years later, this power was to be reactivated. We, along with the rest of humanity, had the opportunity to put right what we had previously done wrong.

Crystals can help us to align with the changes now taking place so that we expand our consciousness and fulfil our greatest potential. Jung said: 'We should not pretend to understand the world only by intellect; we apprehend it just as much by feeling.' Crystals can help us to feel, open our heart to love, restore physical balance, uplift our spirits and bridge the gap between the visible and invisible. They are a vital aid to our evolution into the future and to promote our optimum health now.

8

DREAMS AS KEYS TO EMPOWERMENT

Dreams and crystals in history

Throughout history, dreams, whether from the Bible, poets, authors, mystics and scientists or psychologists, have been used as a source of creative inspiration and knowledge not normally available to the waking mind. In the same way stones too have played a part in our evolution. Mohammed spoke and listened to stones, Moses received the Ten Commandments on stone, Peter was told by Jesus that he was the rock on which the Christian church would be built.

Early scientists such as Nicolaus Steno, a seventeenth-century geologist, and Abbé Haüy, Professor of Numerology at the Museum of National History in Paris in 1784 – who studied stones in the form of crystals – believed they had discovered an aspect of the mind of God, a sense of the underlying order of the universe. They saw the mineral kingdom as a point of communion between man and God, and crystals as the most evolved stone because they reflected more light and were therefore a God-given force to protect against evil.

The function and purpose of dreams

Dreams, though not necessarily a protection against evil, are also a means of communion between man and God. Quantum physics and quantum thinking mean to go beyond what was previously considered normal. Newtonian physics assumed that the basic elements of reality were like tiny bricks, absolutely fixed in number. Quantum physics recognises that its basic elements of neutrons, protons and quarks change all the time. It is an expansion of awareness, a quantum leap into another reality. Dreams and crystals, because they blend the visible and the invisible, bridge both physical and non-physical worlds and can help us make this leap.

Dreams mediate between left and right hemispheres of the brain, logic and intuition, male and female, active and passive, positive and negative. They are a source of power, knowledge, creativity and health. The Talmud says that to ignore a dream is like receiving a letter and leaving it unopened.

When we sleep and dream we are in touch with a wiser, more detached part of ourselves that gives an honest assessment of how we really think and feel as opposed to how we pretend we think and feel in waking life. For example Jeff dreamed of Dolly Parton picking his pockets. When asked what Dolly Parton meant to him he replied, 'a female who uses plastic surgery to retain her sexy image'. When asked who in his life reminded him of Dolly Parton he thought of his girlfriend, who continually borrowed his (plastic) credit cards to buy clothes and pay bills, to improve her appearance, which he considered to be her responsibility rather than his. His dreams made him consciously aware of how upset and frustrated he felt and finally led him to talk to her about it.

To pay attention to dreams is similar to looking at life from a helicopter, instead of driving a car along a road on the ground, where our vision is limited to what is immediately around us. From a helicopter we can see what is going on from a totally different and wider perspective. We can also see what lies behind and what is emerging ahead, we can see the interconnections, the interweaving pattern of events and our place in them. A dream is a psychic reading, our own personal Akashic record. The Akasha is described by some religions as the memory and mind of God. It is the record of everything that has ever happened, written, according to Edgar Cayce, on the invisible 'skein of time and space' in the fabric of the universe.

Dreams allow us to play and experience many roles, and can often solve problems in creative ways that would not have occurred to us in waking life. Numerous dream discoveries have improved our quality of life, both scientifically and artistically. The German chemist, Kekulé, discovered the molecular structure of benzene through his dreams and later, when reporting his findings at a conference, said: 'Let us learn to dream, gentlemen, and then we may find the truth.' Both Harvard Business School and Stanford University have programmes in which businessmen and women are taught to use dreams to solve problems and bring in new ideas.

Dreams reflect and help us to explore – and even change – our innermost beliefs, face our fears, and create new options in our lives. They help us understand ourselves better so that we stop projecting on to others our faults, failures and weaknesses.

Many years ago Freud said that dreams were the Royal Road to the unconscious. Today most psychologists and dream therapists would say that dreams are the Royal Road to life itself and not just tools of diagnosis for the mentally ill. An illustration of this is the American Indian or Australian Aboriginal, who, if separated from his Dreamtime tradition, loses his sense of identity with his family, tribe and community.

Unlike indigenous people who have always valued dreams, omens, visions, hunches and telepathy, and used them as an aid to survival, most of us have learned to deny the value of our own inner wisdom. Instead of relying on our inner senses we switch on the radio or television, or pick up the telephone to obtain information about current events, people and the weather.

These instruments, which so fascinate us, are in reality only outer reflections of the inner abilities we all have. Instead of respecting them, most of us have let them atrophy. As a result we feel cut off from an innate part of ourselves, one another, the Earth and nature. It is not difficult to reawaken these abilities and dreams are one of the simplest, safest and most exciting ways in which to do so.

Working with dreams

1 *Valuing dreams*

The first step in working with dreams is to decide to value them. A dream is part of the psyche's balancing system and as such deserves our respect. Even people who swear they never dream do so four to five times a night and would become psychotic if they did not. In fact the average person spends a third of his life asleep and six years of that dreaming – enough time to graduate as a surgeon, chemical engineer or scientist. What a waste of the brain's potential not to use it during this time.

2 *Preparing for sleep*

The second step is to prepare for sleep. Most of us fall into bed at the end of a long day only to toss and turn, trying to relax. We could sleep better and dream more productively if we did a little groundwork first. Dreaming takes place when our brain-wave rhythm moves from Alpha into Theta, both slower than Beta, the active, decision-making level we use when awake.

Deep breathing, tensing and relaxing our muscles, creative visualisation, listening to music or holding a crystal, all help to put us into Alpha very quickly, which means that we shall be much more relaxed when we get into bed. Creating a peaceful atmosphere in the room around us with flowers, herbs, incense, crystals or candles will also induce deeper sleep and dreams.

If we did no more than mentally honour the night, sleep and dreams, as we got into bed, already the quality of our sleep and dreaming would improve. However, the more effort we put into pre-sleep rites, the more we impress our unconscious, subconscious and higher conscious selves that we are really serious about what we are doing.

Another vital part of sleep preparation is to leave the day behind. No matter what went on, nor what we or anyone else did or did not do, try not to carry the day into the night. We can mentally sum up the day, good, bad or indifferent, and breathe it into a crystal, let it flow out of our feet into the bath or a bowl of water, or into the air in a visionary balloon.

Best of all is to make a note of day-to-day events, especially those with the most emotional impact, the lessons we believe we are meant to learn from them, the people who make an impression on us (good and bad), recurring incidents and general insights. Dreams at night are usually a running commentary on our daily lives – while also reflecting past and future. To keep some sort of record or journal helps us to understand both our dreams and what is going on in our lives at the same time. Before turning out the light do not forget to write down: 'I want to dream and to remember my dream.' This programmes our dreaming selves to respond and can also be used as an affirmation before sleep.

3 Dream recall

The third step in dream work is to learn to recall and record our dreams. Dream recall is an acquired habit and not difficult if we are prepared to practise. Remember that we dream less if we are under a lot of emotional stress, or take pills, drugs or alcohol. Also many of us forget our dreams because we are woken by an alarm or children or by getting out of bed too quickly. Try and wake a few minutes earlier and immediately write down whatever you can recall of your dream.

Never go to bed without leaving pen and pad beside you. If you wake naturally during the night try to write down whatever you can recall of your dreams. You may initially find it easier to speak into a tape-recorder but even if you do, to write a dream down is more powerful. You are literally making the invisible visible – and it affects our consciousness in a different way.

If you wake up with a huge dream scenario that vanishes as you reach for your pad, relax back into the position you were in as you woke; breathe deeply and ask for the dream to come back. If nothing happens roll into a new position. If the dream does not return, simply describe the feelings, the colour of the dream, what you did yesterday, what you felt when you went to bed. It is essential to write something, rather than leave the page a blank. This not only emphasises to your dreaming self the importance you are giving to dreams but will often catalyse your remembering of them.

If the above suggestions do not work for you, you may find taking Niacin and B6 (the mental vitamins) for a short time helpful. A lack of these can also upset our emotional balance. A shortage of B6 makes it difficult to remember dreams. Another catalyst is to drink half a glass of water just before sleep. Affirm, 'I will wake up and I will remember my dreams.' Immediately upon waking, drink the other half and repeat the affirmation. This helps to fix the idea of dreaming in your mind, which like a computer, gives out what you put into it. These steps are simple and they work. However, if you have never paid attention to dreams before, you may have to practise to get results. The most important step is the decision to try and often that alone stimulates a dream.

When writing a dream down note the key symbols first, such as names, numbers, words, plus figures of speech. Often dreamers lose these by concentrating on recording the dream story. Also watch what comes up over the months ahead such as recurring dreams or symbols. Dream symbols disguise feelings. Dream interpretation means translating the picture back to the feeling. This is not difficult. By concentrating on symbols we can merge with them and then discover what they are and where they came from. To observe and contemplate outer life events can lead to similar discoveries that help us understand why our lives unfold in a certain way.

Experiencing and interpreting dreams

People in dreams, even if they appear as the milkman, or the boy or girl next door, should always be interpreted as aspects of oneself first, no matter what secondary meaning they might have. We should look at the quality in us which this person may represent, why is he/she in the dream, what is he or she doing, saying, feeling, and what is this telling us about ourselves? If we have never seen this character before is there anything about him or her that reminds us of someone in our waking lives? In fact, while writing dreams down we should constantly refer back to waking life – what does this feeling, setting, person, activity or symbol remind us of?

We must keep asking questions of ourselves until the answers pop up. It becomes easier and easier with practice. When we have recorded the dream, we should make an intuitive guess at what we feel the dream is saying, its overall meaning for us and our lives, rather than an intellectual interpretation.

Finally we should always decide on what action we are going to take to implement the dream's message. This is an aspect of dreamwork that is often left out. By actualising the dream, even if it is only to wear the colours in it, or contact the person we dreamed about, we draw an energy into our lives that can empower us to live with greater freedom and happiness.

Nightmares and recurring dreams

Never be afraid of what appears in a dream. There is nothing in the unconscious which is not already in life. Any fear or apprehension will often be exaggerated in the form of a monstrous apparition.

The best way of dealing with a nightmare is to get back into it as quickly as possible and face it. Imagine being back in the dream again. Confront the threat, point your finger at it, question it: 'Who are you? What are you? What part of me do you represent? What do you want me to know? – do? How can I help you? Heal you?'

Usually just to face the threat, rather than run away, transforms the energy embodied in the dream image. For example, a friend had recurring dreams in which her husband pushed her overboard into a deep and seemingly bottomless sea. The terror, as she sank deeper and deeper into the water, always woke her.

Guiding her back into the dream, suggesting that she stopped struggling and allow herself to float down into the depths to see either what happened next, or what might be down there, cured her of her fear and stopped the dream recurring. She discovered life in the ocean depths, colourful gardens and a beautiful woman who sang as she handed the dreamer a silver platter of exotic fruit.

Suddenly her husband appeared beside her and they ate the fruit together. She realised that in her previous relationships with men she was so emotional that she drove them away. Now married, she was afraid to show the depth of her feelings in case the same thing happened. Her husband was an emotional man himself, and often unconsciously triggered situations that pushed her overboard, into her feelings.

By going back into her dream she saw now that there were treasures to be gained from letting herself feel deeply and that the depth of these feelings could be expressed (the woman singing) and shared with her husband. In exploring the rich, emotional life of her unconscious she freed a feared, repressed and unlived part of herself. Dreams and imagination can help us all find and heal split-off parts of our personality – often referred to by Jung as our shadow selves.

Nightmares and recurring dreams, which often take nightmare form, are emphatic demands for us to pay attention, a call from our inner to our outer selves to listen, an attempt to wake us from sleep to life. They usually reflect fear, frustration, resentment that our needs are not being met now or were not met in the past, or that something is wrong in our lives. Like all dreams, nightmares and recurring dreams try to point out what we feel and think unconsciously and subconsciously but they do it with an extra kick, which, at the same time, releases a lot of repressed emotional energy.

They often include dreams of being chased; running away and our feet will not move; crying for help and no one answers; taking an exam and our minds go blank; having to give a speech or talk and when we open our mouths no sound emerges, or our notes fly away; falling off a cliff, out of a window, down the stairs or into a black hole; searching in vain for a toilet; walking down the street and our clothes fall off, or we suddenly realise we did not have them on in the first place; our hair and teeth fall out or our faces shatter and disintegrate as we look in the mirror; losing handbags, wallets, money, tickets; missing trains, planes, buses or important appointments; forgetting where we live or where we parked the car. The list is endless and all these dreams are very common. They have an underlying anxiety to them – a fear that, 'I will not appear or perform as I am expected to.'

In all dreams we need to look at how comfortable we were. Did we feel vulnerable, threatened or quite happy when we lost our teeth, changed sex, or sat on the toilet in front of the Queen? During a live radio programme on dreams a young girl phoned in and described a recurring dream in which she saw her own face sporting a luxuriant beard and moustache. I asked her how she felt in the dream. She replied 'Proud. It was only when I woke that I felt concerned and upset.'

I asked her what a moustache and beard meant to her and she said, 'Power, masculinity.' By going through the dream again she realised she could reveal her masculine side with pride, that it was part of, and perfectly balanced with, her femininity. If her entire face had been covered with hair it might have meant she was using male energy, the more assertive side of us, to disguise her femaleness. In fact lots of women do this in life, fearing that to be 'just a woman' is not enough.

Dreams of exposure

So common are dreams of either finding oneself in an unexpected, and usually public place, losing bits of clothing or having them torn off by someone else, that, based on research, an advertising campaign (about thirty years ago) created a promotional idea for women's bras in which the woman's blouse or dress fell away to reveal the bra underneath. The caption said, 'I dreamed I was at the opera . . ., Madame Tussaud's . . ., Kew Gardens . . . or wherever . . . in my XXX bra.' It proved to be one of the most successful advertising campaigns of all time, both men and women relating to it.

Dreams of being naked or semi-naked can symbolise a healthy willingness to 'let it all hang out', to expose freely and express all that we are, or a case of 'I'll show you' almost like a threat. Embarrassment at being naked may signify a fear of exposure, a need to cover up not merely the body but an aspect of one's life we consider shameful.

In dream research women who feel insecure often dream of being abandoned in an unknown area, while men dream of fighting and shooting, desperately trying to establish their identity. Dreams like this indicate a need for help – which usually the dreamer feels is not available. Radio and TV announcers, actors and actresses, frequently dream of either arriving late or forgetting their lines. Aside from indicating an insecurity about what they are doing it can also be a nudge to prepare better for a particular task. This type of dream is also common to ambitious people who feel they cannot quite keep up.

Reducing threats in dreams – and in life

Apart from exploring the dream's message, if we can learn to send love, point a finger, a crystal, a colour, light, or whatever may be meaningful to us, towards the threat it always changes it, either into a smaller version of itself or something quite different. Children who are taught to do this in their dreams learn that in life, by always facing a problem, they can shrink it to a manageable size. We can all do the same.

Connecting to yourself through dreams

In fact children who are encouraged to share their dreams from the moment they can speak tend to become far more verbal, creative, emotionally expressive, and willing to discuss problems as they grow up than children who are not. Research also discovered that heart patients who were taught to use dreams as part of their after-care therapy, which include pre-sleep breathing and relaxation techniques, recovered 60 per cent better than those who decided it was irrelevant.

Pregnant women were also discovered to give birth more easily after using dream-therapy during pre-natal care. Teenagers, when introduced to dreams as part of their curriculum, not only absorbed information better and therefore learned more quickly, but also passed exams more easily. To pay attention, to listen to dreams, means we connect to a wiser and more intelligent self than the one we usually know and use, as well as to an energy that empowers us to behave differently.

There are as many ways of working with dreams as dreams

themselves. These include art, music, mime, dance, acting, drawing, painting, sculpture, gestalt, incubation, dialogue, re-entry as well as writing them down. Remember that the language of a dream is unique and individually tailored for each dreamer. Therefore the more we listen to a dream, immerse ourselves in it, meditate or ponder on it, the more likely it is that the meaning will reveal itself to us. Like learning another language the more we practise it the more proficient we become.

The significance of a dream

People who choose to interpret dreams from a dream dictionary tend to get stuck with the surface meaning, instead of understanding the emotion, or waking life event, that underlies the dream's message. Remember too that each part of a dream has meaning, sometimes more than one. A dream that says one thing today can reveal a completely different idea a few days later.

Dream interpretation should be simple, practical and help us to improve our everyday lives, as well as our understanding of ourselves and others. For me the guarantee of a dream's importance is the emotional impact within the dream and the electrifying burst of energy with which I wake up. Even without specific interpretation I believe that a dream has been understood and integrated when one's life changes as a result. Through dreams and dream incubation (to ask for help, healing or insight) we have available to us an intelligence that can answer any question we may have about life. This intelligence is sometimes called the Higher Self, the Soul, or Super Consciousness. Jung called it the collective unconscious and described it as a human being combining the characteristics of both sexes, transcending youth and age, birth and death and having at his command a human experience of one or two million years. Edgar Cayce referred to it as 'a river of thought, fed by the sum total of man's mental activity since his beginning.'

9

HONOURING
THE EARTH

*In the midst of the garden grew a rosebush, which was
quite covered with roses; and in one of them, the most
beautiful of all, there dwelt an elf. He was so tiny that no
human eye could see him ... oh what a fragrance there
was in his rooms, and how clear and bright were the
walls. They were made of pale pink rose leaves ... What
we call veins on the leaf, were to him high roads and
crossroads ...*

HANS CHRISTIAN ANDERSON, *The Rose Elf*

The ecological crisis

'The world is in one hell of a mess. I think one third of it is now
so far and deeply destroyed that it is going to cost us mega-
billions to put it back into working order.'

So said renowned scientist David Bellamy when speaking at
the Australian Association for Environmental Education Conference back in 1992. Among the many ecological problems he
discussed were cars:

'There are more cars in Los Angeles than in the whole of
China, India, Pakistan, Bangladesh and Indonesia put
together. If cars in Britain reached saturation point it would
require roads, and their parking spaces, the equivalent of a
motorway from London to Edinburgh 944 lanes wide.'

He also spoke of the North Sea's acid rain:

'The north-east coasts of England and the coasts of Europe are now so bad that you can no longer eat the shellfish. The poisons are actually getting into the filter feeders. Not only do poisons go into the foods chain but more acid rain is generated.'

(We need *some* acid rain, but too much, especially from over-entrophication of the sea, destroys trees, which in turn affects the soil, lakes and rivers.)

He had this to say about the Alps: 'One third of all the traffic in Europe squeezes through the Alpine passes, and the resultant pollution is a kind of creeping death that is killing off all the trees.'

'We've got about ten years in which to save the world. If we don't act now, then, within that period of time, many of the earth's species will be extinct,' says Helen Caldicott, MD, founding President of Physicians for Social Responsibility, and member of the 1986 Nobel Prize-winning International Physicians for Prevention of Nuclear War.

'There are only ten thousand elephants left [she continues]. There used to be millions when I was a child. They have become endangered because we like to wear their tusks on our wrists and on our ears. Rain forests are being chopped down to create land to raise cheap beef to give us hamburgers which are no good for our health anyway. We did not evolve eating meat – we evolved eating grain. The amount of grain that is now used in America alone to feed cattle could feed all the starving people in the world. Meanwhile, two-thirds of the world's children are mal-nourished ... The ozone layer is disappearing faster than was predicted. For each 1 per cent decrease in ozone, there is a 6 per cent increase in skin cancer. The dermatologists in Australia have seen a doubling of malignant melanoma in the last ten years.'

Jeremy Rifkin, President of the Foundation for Economic Trends, and of the Greenhouse Crisis Foundation of Washington DC, when discussing the global environmental crisis, said:

> 'Our generation faces the first true global environmental crisis in recorded history. While our ancestors experienced traumatic environmental threats, they were limited to specific geographic regions. Now, as we near the second millennium, a new environmental threat is emerging so enormous in scope that we find it difficult even to fathom. We have no equivalent past experience from which to mount an appropriate response.'

David Bellamy ended up by saying: 'Perhaps this is the kick in the pants we've been waiting for. We've got to start caring for the land. If we don't care for the land the land won't care for us.'

More recently, Lester Brown, President of the Worldwatch Institute in Washington DC, puts the current situation like this:

> 'After millions of years hunting and gathering, and thousands of years tilling the soil, we are entering an era where urban living is the dominant style. This shift has occurred at a breathtaking pace, creating conditions of life as never before.'

Cities are now home to half the world's population and although they take up no more than 2 per cent of the Earth's surface, they use 75 per cent of its resources. In China alone, 300 million people are expected to move into cities by the year 2010. In 1810 the largest city in the world was London with a population of one million. Today, seven million people inhabit London and use 20,000,000 tonnes of fuel; 1,002,000,000 tonnes of water; 2,400,000 tonnes of food. Industrial waste is 11,400,000 tonnes which, combined with 3,900,000 of household waste, is a staggering amount of rubbish to dispose of – only 49 per cent of which is recycled.

No matter how hopeless the situation might seem, Herbert Girardet, Chairman of the Schumacher Society, and author of the *Gaia Atlas of Cities*, believes that urban areas *can* become part of a sustainable future.

How we can help

So, how do we cope, what do we do?

First, we need to focus on what is possible and changeable, rather than on what is impossible and immutable.

The word 'ecology' comes from the Greek word 'oikos', which means 'the household'. Ecological responsibility therefore begins at home. The Earth is dying from global warming, caused by over-use of cars, machinery, electricity and oil. We add to global warming by switching on unnecessary lights, using hair-dryers, air-conditioners, washing machines and electric refriger-ation, as well as plastic containers, spray air deodorants and air fresheners. Newspapers, magazines, packaging and toilet paper are products of trees being cut down without adequate replacement. Much of today's packaging is plastic, which, made from oil, produces almost indestructible toxic waste that no one really knows what to do with.

Maybe our first step is to look at how, individually, we can improve things in a practical way. We can stop blowing our noses on paper tissues, using our cars unnecessarily, and buying products prettily wrapped in five layers of packaging. We could let our hair dry naturally, stop using sprays of any kind, recycle jars, bottles, egg-boxes, newspapers and magazines, use our bathwater for the garden, and stop letting the tap run when we brush our teeth. We should eat simple, non-processed food. If we don't have the facilities to grow our own food we could buy direct from people who do.

Another way we can help to heal the planet is to follow the path of the shaman. A shaman honours the earth as a living being and lets his spiritual or soul self guide his direction through life. Shamanistic teaching demonstrates how we can (and must) live from the heart, balance mind, body, emotion and spirit as well as restore our connection with nature.

While living in America I met and worked with a part native American psychic healer, Joy Messick. She introduced me to the energies inherent in the Medicine Wheel, mandala-type energies that bring us into harmony with ourselves and all of life. I learned to respect the Four Directions, North, South,

East and West, as well as the elements of Air, Water, Earth and Fire.

The powers of the North are to do with the mind and intelligence; the powers of the South stimulate inner knowing, transformation and intuition; the powers of the West deal with stability and physical endurance; the powers of the East lead us to enlightenment through inspiration.

In the book *Where Eagles Fly*, the author Kenneth Meadows suggests that to connect to the powers of the North, we should go outside when the Moon is almost full, face North, align with the North Star and ask to 'be made new'.

To connect with the West we should watch the sun set and 'allow ourselves to be touched by the power that brings change'.

To align with the East we should go outside before daybreak and watch the sunrise. 'As the distant horizon begins to lighten ask the Ravens of the East to enlighten us now ...'

To connect with the South, face South at noon, and draw its power into your life by raising your arm towards the sun and slowly bring it down, while asking for a personal teaching that can make you more intuitive.

If you cannot go outside to do these exercises, I suggest making a circle inside your house, either on paper or with special stones, feathers, leaves and flowers etc., and, using a compass, face North, South, East and West and attune to each direction as you do so.

To connect with the elements of Air, Water, Earth and Fire, it is good to sit by a lake or stream; climb to the top of a mountain and inhale mountain air; plunge your hands into the earth, smell it, get the *feel* of it. Or gaze into the flames of a fire. If this is not possible, simply fill a glass or bowl with water and hold it in your hands, or between your feet on the floor. Imagine the waters of the world, oceans, lakes, rivers, streams and rain, and give thanks for all that flows through them. Every time you splash your face, wash your feet, bath, shower, swim or *drink* it, remember water is the life blood of the Earth and we must respect and acknowledge its capacity to heal and renew us.

Air is as essential to life as water. Correct breathing is a fundamental part of our health and well-being. Stress and anxiety cause many of us to almost stop breathing. 'Inspiration' comes from the Latin 'inspiritus' which means to breathe. To practise conscious breathing, to walk and inhale fresh air, to dance outside on a windy day, or to simply remember the wind blowing through our hair and rustling the leaves on a tree, can all help us attune to the element of Air and connect with its power.

One way to connect to the element of Earth is to stand with bare feet on bare earth or sand (not grass or pavement). Plunge your hands into it – feel the texture and the *energy* of it. Make mud by mixing earth and water and sense that too, either with your feet, hands or imagination. Let it speak to you.

To connect with the element of fire, we must light a fire and gaze into its flames. If this is not possible, light candles. Fire has always been a mixture of god-like magic and means of survival. It can warm, nurture and heal us or cause death and destruction. To gaze into the flames of a bush fire in Australia or a burning hut in an African township literally burns away any false ideas we may have about ourselves.

All these exercises are a wonderfully effective and simple way to help children develop an awareness of the Earth on which they live.

Adjusting to change

While the Earth together with our solar system go through a major transition, every cell in our bodies tries to keep up. Initially it was thought that the brain regulated the immune system but in 1994 scientists discovered that the brain receives a signal from the heart, which in turn responds to a pulse from the Earth, which gets its signal from the sun. Increased solar flares affect the Earth's magnetic fields, which now rotate at a different speed. This means that our hearts now attune to a different pulse and therefore our brain, DNA cells and immune system are undergoing an enormous change. This is why it is far harder to shake off even mild colds and flu. Psychics and clairvoyants have told us of the change to our molecular structure for years and now science explains why, but still the majority of the Earth's population continue to cut themselves off from the Earth and what is happening in, on and to it, by their obsession with money and material possessions.

We are told that the Earth is like a giant crystal such as a geode, with a thin crust and a central core. In an article written by Bob Crane, a friend and co-worker of Marcel Vogel, he says that the three layers of the Earth's interior consist of two spherical shells of crust and mantle and another core sphere. These layers have different levels of rotation which means that they constantly rub against one another as they rotate. This produces large amounts of friction and heat, which melt a portion of the bottom of the crust into volcanic magma. This magma acts as a lubricant between the crust and the mantle. Sometimes it is so great that it rises to the surface of the Earth.

The frictional heat between the core and the mantle results in the stripping away of most of the core's electrons which move to the core-mantle interface. These electrons charge up the mantle, and a low frequency gravitational vibration is produced. Bob Crane says: 'You can see that the interior of the Earth is very precise in its design. If it were not so, our gravitational field would not be constant and the result would be chaos on the surface. This is the situation we may face in the near future.'

We know that nuclear explosions cause huge threats to our atmosphere but today many countries experiment with underground nuclear blasts. The shock waves from every underground nuclear blast eventually create magma-filled fissures, which free the inner earth of excessive internal heat and pressure and also warm the outer atmosphere. An example of this aspect of global warming from the interior of the earth rather than from the sun is the El Nino current produced by an increase of three degrees in the ocean temperature off the coast of western South America.

While crystals can help us attune to the geological changes that occur under our feet (and crystal energy will, I am sure, be used in the future to create gravitational fields of energy to propel space-craft and inter-dimensional communication), we can meanwhile use quantum thinking or mind-power to change and heal the world around us.

However bad all this may appear, we have the power of our minds to change everything around us. Fred Wolf, who wrote the 'Body Quantum', describes the critical nature of consciousness and the role that it plays when connected with matter. Wolf says that we occupy, and create with our minds, a series of patterns of 'quanta energy' which then assemble into energy. These can be released by breath, or by the wilful intention of working with love.

Planting trees

We could also plant trees, which provide oxygen, and of course adequate oxygen is essential for healthy and stable human life. Richard St Barbe Baker, known as the Man of the Trees, and Hans Selye, MD, an expert in stress control, found in experiments on rats that lack of oxygen stimulated violence. A tree planted when a child is born, and dedicated to it, will monitor that child's growth. It will grow, break or bend and shape itself according to what the child experiences as it develops.

The Essene community, to which Joseph and Mary the parents of Jesus belonged, planted a tree for every year of a child's life until it reached maturity. These were probably fruit trees, and no doubt provided a means of support and stability. The Essenes encouraged their children to plant trees. Shouldn't we do the same?

Some years ago a fifteen-year-old schoolboy in Los Angeles decided that the city needed more trees. Near his home was a plot of land on which was an old, disused fire station. He thought that, with the aid of friends, he could fill it with trees and sell them. He approached the local authorities with his idea. They not only refused him permission, but also roared with laughter that a mere schoolboy should even think of anything so crazy. For six years this same boy persevered, contacting local councils, schools, businessmen, politicians, churches and other organisations.

Finally, when he was twenty-one years old, the authorities capitulated and said: 'OK. Do it!' Through this boy's idea, guts and determination a million trees were planted in Los Angeles. If one fifteen-year-old boy can instigate a programme that results in a million trees being planted in a city which desperately needs them why can't we all try to do something similar? Even if each of us does no better than plant one tree a year, the total improvement could be tremendous.

Trees, with their roots in the ground and their branches reaching up into the sky, blend heaven and earth, spirit and matter. In some ancient philosophies the tree was used to illustrate oneness with all of creation. It was a powerful spiritual symbol to study and emulate. Most of us feel completely renewed when we walk through woods and forests, especially the type of forest where the trees are so tall there is almost no light, and the sensation is similar to that of bathing in a cool green pool.

In Russia, Evsei Meilitsev uses the energy of trees to heal his patients. Trees are the balance between heaven and earth. American Indians refer to them as the 'standing people' because of this link. One of Meilitsev's patients, Mikhael, described how trees cured him of rheumatism that was diagnosed when he was eleven years old. After numerous allopathic drugs Mikhael's pain was so acute he could not move without painkillers and antibiotics.

When Mikhael met Evesi he was told to lean against the trunk of an oak tree and draw on its life-energy. Evsei said: 'By leaning against an oak you can revitalise your body and make it resistant to chronic disease. The oak charges you with energy.' Mikhael later reported, 'After a few days I became aware of the energy impact of the trees. I felt energy passing through my head and body and returning to the tree. I felt vibrations at the back of my neck, as if there were a magnet there.'

While an oak charges us, and in the process expands our electro-magnetic field, or aura, a poplar tree draws energy from us. Meilitsev recommends leaning against a poplar to remove 'unhealthy energy' arising from a physical pain or an emotional problem. He has found this to be highly successful in treating diseases such as arthritis and rheumatism. If you prefer to do this in the privacy of your own home, you can apply pieces of poplar tree to afflicted, painful or swollen parts of the body. It appears to work just as well. Remember to re-charge afterwards – either by hugging an oak tree or placing a crystal on the thymus for two to three minutes.

To stand with your bare feet on the ground – preferably grass or earth – and to imagine you *are* a tree, can also revitalise the body. Think of roots flowing from your feet into the depths of the Earth and draw Earth energy into your body. Imagine you have branches that soar into the sky and breathe the energy of sky and sun into your heart and solar plexus.

With your eyes closed, imagine sky and Earth merging together and blending with the essence of your inner being. Whether you do this exercise for five or twenty-five minutes it re-energises mind, body and spirit.

Communication with trees

Trees absorb and transmute our negativities, releasing us from them. Rocks and mountains do the same. Every tree has a spirit, an angel, and all we have to do to communicate with it is to hug it or to sit with our backs against its trunk. Like holding crystals, this is a simple and effective way of revitalising ourselves when we feel tired. If you do this, do not forget to give something back, in the sense of sharing yourself with the tree, and thanking it.

Many years ago, I was in a forest hugging a huge tree, whose trunk was so vast that even with both arms outstretched I could not anywhere near reach round it. After about thirty minutes the tree seemed to speak to me, and said that enormous healing energy was being poured into the Earth at this time, and that all we had to do was to open ourselves to it every day. We would then immediately catalyse healing in everything around us. We did not need to go around deliberately laying our hands on people or things, but rather, before getting out of bed in the morning, to mentally affirm: 'I offer myself as an instrument of healing for whoever and whatever comes into my life today.'

When we do this, we affect everything we touch, from the car we drive to the pavement we tread, and the desk we sit at. I have made a practice of doing this ever since, and feel that I benefit as much as or more than anything or anyone else. I also have three trees which are guardians of my flat when I am away, which is often. When I first moved in, I saw rays of light coming from each tree, forming a triangle of light around the house in which my flat is situated. I acknowledged the spirit of each tree, and when I go away I ask them to hold the light around the house. When I come back I say thank you.

When the storms took place that destroyed much of Kew Gardens, where I live, I had just returned from overseas. It was two in the morning and only on my way back from the airport did I have any idea of how vicious the winds were. I thought 'my' trees would fall right into the house, so I spent hours talking to them. I asked them to lean sideways, to bend with the gale rather than fight against it. Even though trees on either side toppled, tearing out chunks of pavement, leaving a trail of destruction as though bombs had gone off, my guardian trees survived intact.

A French friend, Henri, who has a forest around his house in Provence, goes every day to talk to a particular tree that tells him what to do when things go wrong. Trees, like everything else in nature, will talk to all of us if we listen. An illustration of this is provided by the sacred forest at St Beaume in Provence, leading up to the deep cave in the cliff face where Mary Magdalene is supposed to have spent the last thirty years of her life.

This sacred forest of tall trees of great presence, where hunting has always been forbidden, has been revered throughout the mists of time back to the pre-Christian eras of Druids, pagans and animists. Kings, queens and popes have climbed up through this cathedral of trees, especially around Christmas-time, to pay homage to Mary Magdalene. There are many such natural temples through the world, of configurations of boulders, rivers, forests and rocky bays which we can reconsecrate by our reverence and love. I have never liked to enter the forest of St Beaume without asking permission first, and saying thank you afterwards.

Honouring the Earth

One of the best ways we can all help to re-establish ecological balance is by honouring these natural landscape temples in this way. To take time to be still and listen in such places, as Henri does, will often give us the guidance we need. This guidance may well require us to change things, not just to accept them. In the past many spiritual prophecies concerning the future of a religious group were considered by the prophets who delivered their message to have failed if they came true. A prophecy or prediction was a warning, giving an opportunity for change.

*   *   *

The following speech by Chief Seattle was delivered to Isaac I. Stevens, the new Governor and Commissioner of Indian Affairs for the Washington Territories in December 1854:

'The President in Washington sends words that he wishes to buy our land. But how can you buy or sell the sky? The land? The idea is strange to us. If we do not own the freshness of the air and the sparkle of the water, how can you buy them? Every part of the Earth is sacred to my people. Every shining pine needle, every sandy shore, every mist in the dark woods, every meadow, every humming insect. All holy in the memory and experience of my people.

We know the sap which courses through the trees as we know the blood that courses through our veins. We are part of the Earth and it is part of us. The perfumed flowers are our sisters.

The bear, the deer, the great eagle, these are our brothers.

The rocky crests, the juices in the meadow, the body heat of the pony, and man, all belong to the same family.

The shining water that moves in the streams and rivers is not just water, but the blood of our ancestors. If we sell you our land, you must remember that it is sacred.

Each ghostly reflection in the clear waters of the lakes

tells of events and memories in the life of my people. The water's murmur is the voice of my father's father.

The rivers are our brothers. They quench our thirst. They carry our canoes and feed our children. So you must give to the rivers the kindness you would give to any brother.

If we sell you our land, remember that the air is precious to us, that the air shares its spirit with all the life it supports. The wind that gave our grandfather his first breath also received his last sigh. The wind also gives our children the spirit of life. So if we sell you our land, you must keep it apart and sacred, as a place where man can go to taste the wind that is sweetened by the meadow flowers.

Will you teach your children what we have taught our children? That the Earth is our mother? What befalls the Earth befalls all the sons of the Earth.

This we know: the Earth does not belong to man, man belongs to the Earth. All things are connected like the blood that unites us all. Man did not weave the web of life, he is merely a strand in it. Whatever he does he does to himself.

One thing we know: our God is also your God. The Earth is precious to him and to harm the Earth is to heap scorn on its creator. Your destiny is a mystery to us. What will happen when the buffalo are slaughtered? The wild horses tamed? What will happen when the secret corners of the forest are heavy with the scent of many men and the view of the ripe hills is blotted by talking wires? Where will the thicket be? Gone. Where will the eagle be? Gone. And what is it to say goodbye to the swift pony and the hunt? The end of living and the beginning of survival.

When the last Red man has vanished with his wilderness and his memory is only the shadow of a cloud moving across the prairie, will these shores and forests still be here? Will there be any of the spirit of my people left?

We love this Earth as a newborn loves its mother's heartbeat.

So, if we sell you our land, love it as we have loved it. Care for it as we have cared for it. Hold in your mind the memory of the land as it is when you receive it. Preserve the land for all children, and love it, as God loves us all.

As we are part of the land you too are part of the land. This Earth is precious to us. It is also precious to you. One thing we know: there is only one God. No man, be he Red man or white man, can be apart. We are brothers after all.'

*   *   *

The ecological warnings given to us today by such people as Jonathan Porritt (ex-director of Friends of the Earth), Jeremy Rifkin, Rupert Sheldrake, Helen Caldicott, David Bellamy and many others, including the indigenous peoples worldwide, appear to have a similar base. They urge us to wake up, to stop the exploitation and destruction of the Earth and its atmosphere, to recognise that short-term solutions, like sticking a Band-Aid on an amputated leg, simply do not work, and to accept responsibility and act.

Despite their seemingly pessimistic view of the world, most of these ecological prophets of doom also explain how we can repair the damage. We must stop burning fossil fuels, killing animals for food, stripping nature of its sacred value. We must drop our addiction to unnecessarily sophisticated luxury products, as well as drugs, alcohol and tobacco, and go back to the simple way of life. We must educate our children for the twenty-first century and not the 1800s.

Many of today's children are completely removed from nature. For example, hundreds of children in London had no idea that milk bought in cartons from a supermarket came originally from a cow. When introduced to the process of milking, many of them started to faint. We must dissolve such barriers of ignorance, just as we must wipe out those between races, nationalities, colours, classes and creeds. We should attempt to use our common sense to avoid waste.

David Bellamy described how one of the biggest companies in Germany gives its workers free bus and train tickets as an incentive to leave their cars at home. As a result, the company not only helps to prevent environmental pollution, but also saves money by not having to build parking lots on site. His accountants, said Bellamy, discovered that, by setting light-reflectors on office lights, they save £485,000 in electricity bills every year. He explained that there was enormous investment potential in cleaning up the environment, and that maybe it was this realisation of, 'Oh my God, there's money in ecological awareness!' that would finally push big companies to act in environmentally sensitive ways.

Most environmentalists talk about returning to traditional methods of land care which, developed by indigenous peoples for thousands of years, are in complete harmony with the Earth. There is an immense wealth of wisdom in indigenous peoples, especially that which is being recognised in the American Indians and Australian Aboriginals, which we should tap into. David Bellamy did not advocate a return to the land as a retrograde step, but as a modern way to manage the world's natural resources. In discussing current problems he said that it was only through communities working, thinking and talking together, that these problems would be overcome. All we need is the will to act. Clearly, some of the possible solutions are going to force us to make choices about our current and future lifestyles.

For most of us, this means we must explore ways in which we can simplify our lives and become collectively more self-sufficient. We must ask ourselves: 'Do I have a God-given right to eat the flesh of animals bred on battery-farms who in most cases are killed with unbelievable cruelty?'

Releasing animals' spirits

In the 1970s I worked with a great teacher, Alan Chadwick. Alan had been a Shakespearean actor before he became a gardener and spiritual teacher. He created magnificent gardens all over the world, and taught his students the philosophy of life through nature and the garden. No student was allowed to eat meat unless he or she was prepared to kill the animal. Most of his students became vegetarians, but he showed those who chose not to how to kill a chicken or a sheep with consciousness, with love. This means we talk to the spirit of the animal first, tell it what we are about to do, and thank it. When this is done the spirit of the animal leaves its body before it is killed.

When one animal kills another, there are special devas – or angels – belonging to the animal kingdom who anaesthetise it. Our system of meat production and mass slaughterhouse murder interferes with this process and causes the animal's body to fill with fear, thus creating toxins which in turn affect our bodies when we eat unconsciously butchered meat. Muslims understand these truths. Their *halal* meat means that the animal has been killed in a specific and merciful way, to allow its spirit to escape.

We can alleviate some of this by blessing our food and offering our bodies as a means of transmutation to another level of every kind of food we eat, not just meat. Fifteen years ago I was involved with a group of doctors who decided to test the effects of various methods of cooking on foods. These experiments included frying, grilling, baking, use of microwave ovens, as well as the use of aluminium foil, and of blessing food once prepared. Microwave ovens tended to kill the lifeforce, aluminium foil markedly to diminish it, while blessing food restored much of its vitality. To pass a crystal over food either while cooking it or before eating it has the same effect. Similar benefits follow if we cook with care and love.

Several years ago, many of my clients and workshop participants felt a strong desire to eat meat. Most of them had been vegetarians for years; some of them had never ever tasted meat. All of them expressed concern that to give in to the craving would somehow lead them away from the spiritual path they believed themselves to be on. I noticed the craving was especially strong in therapists who used various forms of bodywork such as massage, Alexander technique, aromatherapy, rolfing, reflexology etc., in their therapeutic sessions. During a meditation I asked what I perceive to be my spiritual helpers why this was happening. I was told that because our DNA/molecular structure together with our immune system was changing, many people needed to eat more protein, even if it was animal protein. I was also told that the vibrational shifts could give us an unconscious urge to anchor or ground ourselves and to eat meat or fish was one of the ways to do so.

I was myself a vegetarian for nearly twenty years and recently suddenly craved steak, so I ate it (two or three times). A few years ago this would have been a physical and mental impossibility. I felt fine. During my vegetarian days my basic diet was raw food and vegetables, no cheese or eggs. I now eat fish and love it and if my body craves the occasional piece of chicken I eat it.

I believe that as we move into the next millennium, we will (and must) eat natural, simple food such as organically grown fruit, vegetables, seeds, seaweeds and grains. Eventually we will not eat food at all, but will absorb from the atmosphere the nutrients we need and later still we will mentally create anything we desire.

Meanwhile our current reality is such that many people automatically eat animal flesh. I believe we must move beyond the judgement that this is right or wrong. Planet Earth has been a school of duality – I learn to value the positive by experiencing the negative. In other words, I value food, by not having enough to eat, I value freedom through imprisonment. The imprisonment can come from illness, authority or severe family or work control, not just being in goal.

Making a start

We must also ask ourselves if we have the right to ski in the Alps, if our presence there, and the building of elaborate hotels and ski-lifts, help to create erosion, which in turn causes avalanches that destroy even more trees, and subsequently the air we breathe. Do we have an automatic right to use cars so excessively, when we know that the resultant pollution adds to thermal heat expansion, one of the causes of our currently fluctuating weather patterns, and a possible cause of melting ice-caps, rising sea levels, and future tidal waves?

In other words, making choices about our current and future lifestyles means we must become totally aware of the laws of cause and effect. It also means our moving from individuality – I – (illness begins with i) to universality – we (wellness begins with we). It is not always possible to change everything at once, especially if we have forgotten that our limited human consciousness has powers once accorded to the gods. We can start by recognising that each one of us can make a difference and that the time is ripe for us to do so.

Aside from practical decisions, such as not to waste food, to pass on unused items of clothing, goods and utensils, and sometimes to walk instead of riding by car, we can all help to transform the environment by picking up litter where we find it in front of us – especially when it is a Coca-Cola can or discarded sweet wrapper halfway up a mountain, or in the grass when we walk the dog. We can decide to admire wild flowers and leave them there for the next person to admire too, instead of picking them.

Water: the blood of Gaia

In Bulgaria, the students of Beinsa Douna were taught never to pass a mountain stream or spring without making sure that the water ran freely. They learned that water was sacred, the blood of Gaia or Mother Earth, and that it contained within it elements to heal mind, body and spirit. During one of my own visits to Bulgaria I developed altitude sickness in the mountains. Two of Beinsa Douna's women disciples, now eighty-five years old, came to my tent and, through gestures, because we did not understand one another's languages, urged me to take off my clothes and to drink pints of hot water while they massaged me from head to foot with more hot water.

I began to feel even worse, but the two women insisted on pouring more water down my throat while they frenziedly rubbed my body. Eventually they wrapped me in blankets and told me to relax and try to sleep. I sweated and dozed, dozed and sweated. The women returned and administered more of their hot water treatment. They did this three times, after which I recovered completely.

I have seen and experienced water used as a healing treatment hundreds of times. For colds, 'flu, and even emotional depression, the same treatment was applied. Cold water compresses, such as ice wrapped in a face cloth, were applied to the wound or broken bone, followed immediately by hot water. This alternating therapy will release the muscle spasm often caused by pain.

Drinking warm water first thing in the morning and last at night not only clears the blood and organs of the body, but also clears away any blockage between our physical and etheric bodies. I used to suffer from migraine headaches and, apart from dealing with the cause (conflict with authority, my own as well as others, I found that to apply a wet pad, as hot as I could bear it, over my eyes and forehead, released the tension by relaxing the constriction of the blood vessels in the area that caused pain.

To drink lots of water is a simple way of clearing our bodies of toxicity and will, I believe, be acknowledged as the major medicine of the future. To revere water means not only to be aware of how we use it, and what it can be used for, but also to be willing to clear streams, ponds, fountains and rivers when they become blocked. As when releasing a constriction in the physical body, or the circulation, by doing this we help the Earth's energy to circulate more freely. We are also then more attuned to the present Age of Aquarius, whose sign is the waterbearer.

For eons the waters from holy springs such as Lourdes and Glastonbury have cured hundreds and thousands of people. More recently water from Japan is becoming known as a cure for various ailments. Because the pharmaceutical companies tend to suppress this knowledge, very little is known about it. When I asked a Japanese healer for more information he smiled and said that I could taste the water myself. He filled a glass from the tap and held it in his hands for a few seconds before passing it to me to drink. The water tasted like bubbling spring water and I felt immediately energised. The point he was making was that we can do so much for ourselves if we put our consciousness into what we do. We do not need to go to Japan or Timbuctoo to find miraculous cures. This same healer asked me if I liked fresh air and when I replied 'Yes,' he passed his hands over my face and a gust of fresh air filled my nostrils. 'Do you like roses, incense, the smell of leaves?' he questioned, and when I nodded yes, his hands transmitted each fragrance. He believes these skills are entirely normal and available to everyone if we literally put our minds to them.

Angels, devas and fairies

One of the most devastating results of man's 'fall from grace' was the split between the human, the angelic and the elemental kingdoms. At the beginning of time, man walked the Earth with the ability to commune with angels and elementals: devas, fairies and nature spirits, mermaids and mermen. Gradually this ability was lost and mankind not only forgot how to work in conscious co-operation with these realms, but also began to perceive the nature kingdom as devoid of intelligence. In order to truly transform and heal the Earth we must also heal the schism, the separation between humanity and these other levels of intelligence.

For hundreds of years we have seen fairies (or faeries) depicted either in semi-human form, with gossamer wings and tiny, delicate bodies, clad in shimmering diaphanous gowns, or as Snow White type dwarfs, squat, ugly and big-nosed. According to the men and women who have personal contact with the faerie kingdom, 'a faerie is not a diminutive winged pre-pubescent girl hovering over the hedgerows' but rather 'a tall, beautiful, shining being, lit by an inner radiance'. These spirits will disguise themselves as ugly, witch-like old women to test the kindness and love, the true nature of the people they reveal themselves to. They will often appear at the side of a lake, stream or pool – they may ask directions, or give them, and as we turn back to wave farewell, there is no one there.

I believe that faeries – whether gnomes, elves or water-sprites – have a background connection to God, the Sun, the Moon and the stars, and have chosen 'earth-work' to help humanity re-connect to its own divinity.

According to Hugh Mynne (author of *The Faerie Way*), today's message from the elemental kingdom is that in order to resonate fully to the pure harmonics of light, we must absorb or 'eat' our shadow. The green world *minus* the shadow self, equals 'faerieland'. When we release the energy held back by the shadow, it spirals back to the primal song (or source of life) and the meaning is restored. Hugh Mynne describes the people of the Earth as being in a deep shadow initiation –

'viewing themselves in the black obsidian mirrors of the underworld'.

Many films and television programmes force us to confront our deepest fears and guilts, in other words, our shadow selves. The collective message from the elementals is that we must take responsibility for *all* of our world. 'If we hear of a famine, even if it is halfway across the world, we must cultivate generosity. If we hear of the bigotry of others we must strive to be more tolerant ourselves; if we hear of atrocities, instead of dehumanising the perpetrators, we must ensure that we are free of all aggressive thoughts. Only in this way can harmony be restored. Person, land and planet are parts of one whole and we must heal the whole.'

Contacting the elemental kingdoms

To re-awaken our sensitivity to the elemental beings, and to nature itself, we must be open, receptive and loving toward whatever we wish to make contact with. Love is the open sesame to all the invisible realms. We must also drop any prejudice (such as 'this is rubbish'), fear of the unknown, which often creates blocks and boundaries (even in meditation) and be willing to listen with both inner and outer ears.

To begin with we can simply talk to the plants, trees, flowers and even household equipment around us. Thank them all for the work they do, the joy they give, the beauty they reflect. If a tree or bush is going to be pruned or cut down, tell it and its helpers that this will happen a few days before it is done. This allows the flower faeries and nature spirits to withdraw their energy. All elementals love light, colour, music and brightness, so to encourage their presence in our lives, we should create this kind of atmosphere in our houses and gardens. If we wear light, happy clothes, faeries and elves are more likely to respond. They love children and happy people, so the more childlike we can become, the more heartful we are, the more we inspire elemental contact.

Always leave a corner of the house and garden available for them. The garden space, however small, should be uncultivated, a little wild. The indoor space should be spotlessly clean, with a few fresh flowers, candles, crystals and anything else that has particular meaning for you. Both in my house and garden, I say aloud: 'This is especially for you – your own sacred space – and I invite you to use it whenever you want to.' Sometimes I see a flash of light, a movement out of the corner of my eye or hear a faint sound of music or bells – even my own name called.

For deeper contact, remember that, as with angelic communication, dawn, midday, dusk and midnight are times when the veils between dimensions are thinner and therefore communication easier. Rose quartz and Phantom crystals also facilitate our ability to work with faery realms, as does the state of altered consciousness that comes through meditation and deep relaxation. To attune to anything we need to first concentrate and focus all our attention on it with our eyes open, then contemplate it in a more relaxed fashion before we visualise or imagine it with eyes closed. Allow whatever thoughts, words, or feelings that arise in your mind's eye to float up without judging them. Later you may want to write down, paint, or draw any feelings, inspiration or information that comes to you as a result of this experience. You will find, as Wordsworth wrote in *Intimations of Immortality*, '. . . the meanest flower that blows can give thoughts that do too often lie too deep for tears . . .'

Healing the inner and outer worlds

Jonathan Porritt says: 'Ecology is a process of healing, a way of providing meaning to an otherwise sterile and empty world . . .' No matter how simple the first ecological steps we take are (and of course there are hundreds more than the ideas I have mentioned) they will help us to move beyond our material confines, and recognise that we are strands in a miraculous web of creation connected to the source of life itself.

When we live this awareness, we jump into the magical world of quantum living, thinking and being. This quantum leap into another reality is not only an expansion of consciousness that recognises oneness in all of creation, but also dissolves the barriers between the visible and invisible, time and space, spirit and matter. Similar to the awakening of Kundalini conscious-ness, through its leap of energy from the base to the crown chakras, quantum thinking steps up life on to its next evolutionary level, gives birth to what Jean Houston called 'the Possible Human' and Paul Solomon described as 'the Meta-Human'. Both are descriptions of men and women who have thrown off the shackles of past conditioning, the brainwashing that said that there was only one way to think, which did not include imagination, intuition and inspiration.

Great scientists and inventors, such as Edison, Einstein and Tesla, many musicians, writers and artists have all demonstrated the qualities of the Possible and Meta human being, who easily moves far beyond what was previously considered normal. The Tibetan lamas, who can sit naked in the snow and melt it by using the power of their minds and imagination, bilocate – appear in many different places at once – and cover huge distances by leaping through the air, also demonstrate these qualities.

St Teresa, among many other saints, was an exceptional human being. She could levitate, and had visions which inspired her to live in a certain way. One day one of her nuns, while scrubbing the chapel floor, floated up to the ceiling. St Teresa sharply called her back, saying: 'This is not an excuse to get out of scrubbing the floor!' All these people were quantum thinkers who, in mastering the laws of time and space, recognised that there were no limitations to what a human being could do or be, provided his belief was strong enough.

Edison used to fast and go without sleep for days in order to reach a point of light-headedness in which the answers he needed would come. Einstein lulled himself into a similar state by gazing at clouds, while Tesla not only saw ideas in the air but wrote them there himself when he needed to remember them. Today we do not even need to make special efforts to attain this new level of creativity. The current epoch is already pushing us into it.

Nuclear evolution

In the 1960s Christopher Hills, PhD, author of *Nuclear Evolution* and many other books, used this title to describe the evolution of consciousness, the development of the human mind

to its fullest potential, and the recognition that human consciousness affects the atomic, molecular structure of the universe.

Nuclear evolution is another way to describe quantum
thinking, or the way that energy follows thought, and shows us
that we not only create our own reality, but that with a snap of
the imagination, can change it. To live in this way is similar to
living inside a hologram. We see the whole picture instead of
part of it. It is like being the writer, producer and director of a
movie with an overview of the plot, instead of being stuck in the
role of an actor in it. If we decide it is not going to be a box-
office success, we can re-write the script.

To understand that we have the power to change whatever we
do not like about our present circumstances is tremendously
exciting. It is also frightening, because of the responsibility it
brings. In the brilliant Dave Clark musical *Time*, Akash, played
by Laurence Olivier, says: 'Look at what you are thinking. See
the pettiness and the envy and the greed and fear, and all the
other attitudes that cause you pain and discomfort ... If you
truly want to change your world, my friends, you must change
your thinking.'

Visualising the new world into being

Outside world events are simply a reflection of our internal
states of mind. Our thoughts have creative power, which in the
past we have used or directed unconsciously. The new world we
are stepping into is one in which the power of thought and
imagination, the inter-relatedness between consciousness and
matter, will be demonstrated and worked with.

This means that no matter how dismal the current state of the
world is, we have the power to change it without even getting
out of bed. To know this is more important than any other
discovery we have made. In other words, if we give some time
and energy to managing and directing our consciousness
towards the positive instead of the negative, we can turn the
world around. To do this, we should focus on whatever may
concern us, and visualise or imagine it in a different light.

For example, if we are worried about certain animals
becoming extinct, we should see them as healthy and happy,

adapting to a changing world instead of being annihilated by it. We ought, however, to remember that every few thousand years it may be that some species have completed their cycle of evolution on this planet, like the dinosaur. We should bless them, love them, and release them, in the same way as we might do when someone close dies.

Instead of feeling horror at the latest incident of conflict in the world, we should visualise enemies becoming friends, and send thoughts of peace, forgiveness and compassion towards anyone who fights a war, visualising them becoming tired of hurting one another, and moving forward into a new era of understanding and co-operation.

Instead of worrying about holes in the ozone layer, it is better to imagine them knitting together, after we have taken all possible practical steps to aid this. Maybe we should look at the possibility that these holes symbolise a need for us to open windows in our mind to an awareness of other planets and galaxies, thus moving towards a cosmic, instead of our merely individualistic, consciousness. Think of government and other leaders making decisions that benefit the whole of mankind instead of small nationalistic parts of it. Whether it is a dying species, a starving population, warring factions, disaster victims, governments or Earth changes that affect us, we can still do something about it, even from a distance.

O Great Spirit whose voice I hear in the winds
whose breath gives life to the world – hear me.
I am small and weak
I need your strength and your wisdom.

May I walk in beauty.
May my eyes ever behold the red and purple sunset.

Make my hands respect the things you have made
and my ears sharp to hear your voice.
Make me wise so that I may know
the things you have taught your children
the lessons you have hidden in every leaf and rock.

Make me strong, not to be superior to my brothers,
but to be able to fight my greatest enemy . . . myself.
Make me ever ready to come to you with straight eyes
so that when life fades as the fading sunset
my spirit will come to you without shame.

PRAYER OF THE SIOUX PEOPLE

Another potent exercise is to visualise the planet encircled with light, or to offer it, and everything and everyone on it, into the hands of God, with the thought that all is unfolding exactly as it should, whether we, from our relatively limited human perspective, can understand it or not. The Earth is the greatest school of all time, providing billions of different lessons and opportunities. It is a planet of duality, which teaches us the positive through the negative; if I need to learn to value my health, I may choose to occupy a body that is sick. If I need to appreciate peace, I may do so through war; freedom through years of imprisonment.

We can also do a tremendous amount, both individually and collectively, through prayer; simply say: 'Thy will be done!' A beautiful prayer for these times is the well-known Great Invocation:

From the point of Light within the mind of God
Let light stream forth into the minds of men.
Let Light descend on Earth.

From the point of Love within the Heart of God
Let love stream forth into the hearts of men.
Let Christ return to Earth.

From the centre where the Will of God is known
let purpose guide the little wills of men –
The purpose which the Masters know and serve.

From the centre which we call the race of men
Let the Plan of Love and Light work out.
And may it seal the door where evil dwells.

Let Light and Love and Power restore the Plan on Earth.

Instead of watching TV in an empty-minded way, we could practise doing so consciously. In other words, project loving thoughts towards the actors, announcers and newscasters; imagine that all the people who watch and listen benefit in some way.

The power of thought is limitless. I once worked in America with Olga Worrell, a well-known healer, in experiments to test her mental force. In front of our eyes, she changed and dissolved cloud formations, appreciably improved the quality of food, water and wine, and made plants grow faster and bigger. Every one of us has something of this power. If we used it together, we could achieve miracles.

The invocations of the Essenes

Many spiritual groups before us have had this mastery. Edmond Bordeaux Szekely's book *The Gospel of the Essenes*, which he translated from the original Hebrew and Aramaic of the Dead Sea Scrolls, says that there are three paths leading to truth. The first is the path of consciousness, the second that of nature, and the third the path of accumulated experience of earlier generations, passed down through literature, art and music. He says, like many scientists and biologists today, that consciousness is the most immediate reality for us which contains the keys to the universe.

The Essenes were a brotherhood particularly strong in the last centuries before Christ and the first century AD. They lived simple lives on the shores of lakes and rivers, grew their own food, studied the laws of healing, astrology and prophecy. They were physically strong and psychologically healthy. Basic to the Essene way of life was their daily communion with the heavenly Father and earthly Mother, which they did by attunement through a special angel at dawn and dusk. The evening angel was connected to the heavenly Father and the morning one to the earthly Mother.

I have practised and shared these daily invocations for at least thirty years, and found them to be a beautiful, simple and powerful way of moving through the week. The Essene tree of life sets out these angelic forces, beginning with Friday night, as follows:

Friday night		The Father and I are one
Saturday	a.m.	Greetings to the earthly Mother
	p.m.	Angel of Eternal Life
Sunday	a.m.	Angel of Earth (Regeneration)
	p.m.	Angel of Work and Creativity
Monday	a.m.	Angel of Life
	p.m.	Angel of Peace
Tuesday	a.m.	Angel of Joy
	p.m.	Angel of Power
Wednesday	a.m.	Angel of Sun
	p.m.	Angel of Love
Thursday	a.m.	Angel of Water
	p.m.	Angel of Wisdom
Friday	a.m.	Angel of Air

The Essenes also communed with the stars, trees, nature, the different phases of the moon, and the spiritual brotherhood of the Children of Light. To invoke these angelic forces as they did is another way of helping to restore the relationship between Heaven and Earth, and will strengthen, guide and spiritually sustain us, so that instead of feeling like strangers in a foreign land we can enjoy the wonders of creation.

Invoking angels

Another powerful and magical way to greet each day is to invoke an angel to inspire, guide, protect, support, heal or even help us with a particular task. Simply close your eyes and call forth the angel you most need in the moment. For example, I might call upon the Angel of Inspiration before writing a book; the Angel of Communication before giving a talk; the Angel of

Courage before going to the doctor or dentist; the Angels of Peace and Patience if I'm driving in a traffic jam. Before any car journey I always invoke the Angels of Traffic to clear the way and lead me to the correct destination without getting lost. This also helps me find a parking space when I need it! I ask the Angels of Efficiency to help me organise and tidy the house, Angels of Beauty and Joy to help me arrange flowers . . . and so on.

Instead of naming an angel, you might want to simply ask which angel chooses to spend the day with you. This can be done in the moment, with your eyes closed during a meditation, or by choosing an angel card. Findhorn have a wonderful set of angel-cards, which are available in many bookshops, or you can make your own by writing various names on small pieces of cardboard. (Don't forget to ask the angels of Creativity and Inspiration to help you.)

Whether we see or sense the angelic realms or not, rest assured they are active in every aspect of our lives. Each house, village, town and country has its own angelic presence – the larger the area the more angels there are giving their invisible support.

If you have never done this before, you may find the following suggestions helpful:

1 Write a letter to an angel and ask it to reveal itself to you.

2 Ask an angel to come into your dreams.

3 Apply the Aura Soma No. 37 oil before you invite an angel into your life. This violet/blue fragrant oil is called 'The Guardian Angel Comes to Earth'. You could also use No. 44, which is pale lilac and blue and named 'The Guardian Angel'.

4 Close your eyes and relax your body. Do this by breathing slowly and deeply while you tense and tighten each muscle in your body and then, one by one, relax them. Imagine a light from your heart expanding to encompass your entire body. Take a few moments to be at peace with yourself. You can do this exercise in the house or outside in nature. Keep your eyes closed and visualise an angel standing in front of you.

What would it look like? What would it say to you? What would you like to say or ask for? Maybe words will pop into your mind, or you will feel bathed in love. Use your creativity and imagination. If you practise this for fifteen to twenty minutes every day you will begin to consciously experience an angelic presence.

5 Follow the same basic relaxation method but now imagine that you are wandering in a lush and beautiful garden, or strolling up a hill, in search of the angel you have chosen to call upon. Imagine it appearing before you and that you can reach out and hold hands. Know that this is a beloved friend that you can talk to about anything in your life, without apology or explanation. At the end you may want to write down any thoughts or feelings that come to you.

Before any of these exercises, I always cleanse my aura, either by following the technique on p. 199 or by visualising myself bathed in colour or light. I find the Aura Soma pomanders excellent for aura-cleansing too. (In fact they are so powerful that five minutes after applying one of the pomanders before a plane trip the man next to me said that my aura was 'pushing him off his seat'.)

No matter what method you choose to contact an angel, always remember to acknowledge its presence, bless and say thank you – even if, initially, you experienced very little. I promise that if you persevere, you will not only sense and know when angels are around, but also your whole life will change. Remember too the words of Antoine de Saint-Exupery: 'It is only with the heart that one can see rightly; what is essential is invisible to the eye.'

Part Three

THE MAGIC OF
CREATIVE LIVING

10

OUT OF
THE SHADOWS

To move fully into the magical world of creative living, and to enjoy its wonders, we must drastically alter our perceptions of reality, and drop the crippling thought patterns of the past, which have caused us to feel separate, isolated and helpless.

We have to stop looking at everyday life as if it were the only reality. The pictures flickering on the screens of our mind are no longer the only truth. Our situation is like that of a child who watches a movie and sees it as absolutely real, instead of a projection of celluloid images on a screen. As an adult he recognises the source of the scene, the rehearsals and dress-rehearsals of words and actions, that are finally reflected before him like a mirror-image of what was originally set in motion.

In his *Republic* Plato describes people who, living inside a cave, could only see shadows reflected on a wall by the flickering flames of a fire, which they assumed to be real. Eventually some of them leave the cave and go outside, where they see a different world, which includes shadows on the ground from the sun, and ultimately the sun itself. Full of excitement, they rush back to tell the others all about what they have discovered, only to be laughed at and told they are crazy. Those within the cave prefer to be imprisoned or chained by their illusions of what is real. It is safe, comfortable, and familiar.

Awakening to change means that we must break the chains that bind us to the conviction that we are born miserable sinners full of guilt, fear and self-contempt. Like the people imprisoned in Plato's cave, most of us are so afraid of life itself that we only just exist, trapped in a shadow-land that is so stifling that we never claim our right to live fully and joyously. The new epoch drags us by the scruff of our necks out of this shadow-land and into one of play, excitement and adventure.

Lack of self-love

During my counselling sessions I have found that the basic common denominator to the problems that beset humanity is lack of self-love. It is the prime saboteur of human happiness – the wound that can create dysfunctional people who reach for drugs and alcohol to numb the pain. If we do not love and accept ourselves, nothing works. We blame others for what goes wrong in our lives, put the responsibility for our happiness and unhappiness on other people, try to be what we imagine they want us to be, instead of accepting ourselves exactly the way we are.

When we live like this it is not only sad, but exhausting, as if we were blowing up a life-size balloon, and had to keep it full of air. Every now and then we get distracted and look away, which causes the balloon to deflate, so we frantically puff more air into it. This balloon of 'false image' comes from the fear that who I really am *is* who I fear I really am. In other words, I am not so crash-hot as a personality, so I had better create a nicer me. This separates us from our real selves, from life, from people and happiness. It is time to let the balloon deflate itself and fly away.

Much of our lack of self-worth stems from the fact that parents tend to give love to their children when their behaviour and performance fits the parents' demands, and withdraw that love when they do not. This teaches us that love, acceptance or approval are conditional on how we behave or perform, instead of being unconditional for who we are.

Whether parents or not, how many of us freely let the people in our lives be who they are, and not who we want them to be? How many of us say, 'I'll love you, provided you love me'? Or 'I'll love you provided you conform to what I demand that you do' – such as come home on time for the delicious meals I prepare, weed the garden, empty the rubbish, and pay all the bills' – or, from the husband's viewpoint, to have prepared delicious meals on time, to take care of the children, to dress seductively at all times, and to be an unfailing source of support.

Unconditional love is the recognition in the other of the divine. It does not mean acceptance of conscious and consistent cruelty by others, but rather to separate a person from what he or she does. In other words, the divine in me acknowledges the divine in you, even if I do not always like or approve of what you do.

Most religions teach us that self-love leads to egotism, yet without self-love we do not have the confidence to enjoy life, make mistakes and correct them without punishing ourselves, or love others easily, without fearing that our love will not be returned. Religion also teaches us that we are all sparks of God and therefore perfect, while at the same time filling us with fear and guilt for being miserable sinners. To love and accept ourselves totally as we are now does not mean that there is no room for future improvement. However, we have no need to seek excessive perfection, any more than we should condemn ourselves too ruthlessly. We should live comfortably in the middle, perfectly whole, not wholly perfect.

Orthodox religion often injects guilt in children. For example, my convent school education taught me that I was the worst child ever born and that God was a bad-tempered, judgemental, and terrifying old man with a beard, who had nothing better to do day and night but to peer accusingly at me from the clouds, where he chalked up all my transgressions. I was told that the good died young because God loved them and wanted to live with them. I would therefore live to a ripe old age. I learnt that I was the rotten apple who would contaminate all the other apples, and would inexorably end up living at the devil's right hand.

During one particularly difficult term I was discovered with a book entitled *Beauty Hints from the Stars* which I had secreted between the covers of my mathematics exercise book. I was locked up in the Mother Superior's study for three days while every nun who taught in the school, as well as the two hundred from the convent, came one by one to tell me what an evil and unforgivable sinner I was.

In fact, the book had a picture of Marilyn Monroe on the cover, and the beauty tips inside were of a fairly innocuous nature. They revealed that Lana Turner rubbed her elbows with lemon rinds, Doris Day washed her hair with camomile tea, while Marilyn Monroe herself used cucumber face masks to keep her skin looking good. It was only years later that I discovered that Marilyn Monroe was thought to be wicked because she had dared to pose naked for a photo – although she certainly was not naked in this book.

This convent school indoctrinated me with the belief that no matter what I did I was an instrument of the devil and would 'come to no good'. The nuns instilled in me a paralysing fear of authority and of making mistakes, as well as such a deep sense of guilt, that even today I am often the one who apologises when someone else pushes a supermarket trolley over my feet, or drops tea over my skirt. In the past I used to be the sort of person who would come home from a hard day's work, sit down to catch my breath, and if my son or husband came into the room, leap to my feet, apologise for just sitting, and explain that I was just about to prepare dinner, water the garden, or walk the dog.

If someone said: 'You look wonderful, what a pretty dress!' instead of saying 'Thank you' I would apologise, describe the bags under my eyes, and add that I had bought the dress ten years ago secondhand. I had so little self-worth that I virtually apologised for the air I breathed. Guilty people become perfectionists. They explain, justify and apologise for every action they take. Unable to give love and approval to themselves, they seek it from others, and often end up in the 'poor little me' martyr syndrome, while life passes them by.

I am sure that the nuns at my convent genuinely believed that by making me feel guilty they improved my character. In fact, as Paul Solomon says, if guilt is made obsessional, by far its most likely effect is to make the sufferer commit exactly the same supposed crime again. If guilt has any virtue at all, it is simply to give us a little nudge, a tap on the shoulder, to point out that we have made a mistake. There is no sense in using guilt for self-destruction. Yet many of us, myself included, have without reason been immobilised by guilt for most of our lives.

Fear, like guilt, can paralyse. Children need to learn to respect the fact that some things may harm them, such as fast traffic on highways, swimming pools and high seas (especially if they cannot swim), fierce dogs or other hostile animals. Respect is very different from fear. Children who are taught to fear, in the belief that it protects them from what they fear, often lose their sense of adventure, their motivation to touch, taste and try. Parents can, by their own example rather than words, show their children that life does not have to be a series of worries about finance, health, safety and the future, but should be a miraculous and wonderful opportunity to grow and evolve. The following words from a poster entitled 'Children Learn What They Live' perfectly sums this up:

If a child lives with criticism, he learns to condemn.
If a child lives with hostility, he learns to fight.
If a child lives with ridicule, he learns to be shy.
If a child lives with shame, he learns to feel guilty.
If a child lives with tolerance, he learns to be patient.
If a child lives with encouragement, he learns confidence.
If a child lives with praise, he learns to appreciate.
If a child lives with fairness, he learns justice.
If a child lives with security, he learns to have faith.
If a child lives with approval, he learns to like himself.
If a child lives with acceptance and friendship, he learns to find
  love in the world

In Khalil Gibran's book *The Prophet* he says in response to woman's question about children:

Your children are not your children.
They are the sons and daughters of Life's longing for itself.

They come through you but not from you,
And though they are with you yet they belong not to you.

You may give them your love but not your thoughts,
For they have their own thoughts.
You may house their bodies but not their souls,
For their souls dwell in the house of tomorrow, which you
    cannot visit, not even in your dreams.
You may strive to be like them, but seek not to make them like
    you . . .

The lost inner child

No matter how far removed our childhood was from these
ideals, most of us had parents who did the best they could for us
at the time. Most of us who have children do likewise. We fall
into parenting without training or qualification, so despite how
perfect we may try to be, or how happy our family life is or was,
there will usually be something missing. We tend to identify
more with the something missing, or what was not there in the
form of love, care and support, than with what *was* there. The
result is that many of us have an inner 'lost child' who, angry,
afraid, unhappy or forgotten, clamours for attention, and
demands that all its unfulfilled needs from the past are taken
care of. This inner child's hunger for love can affect, and even
destroy – if ignored – the balance of our lives today.

My own lost inner child, believing it could never win,
stimulated the desire in me to prove I could. Consequently I
worked almost twenty hours a day for months at a time, until
this neglected child, who needed some play and fun, rebelled. I
would then collapse in a heap, throw up my 'responsible' job –
which was usually creative and enjoyable, as well as highly
competitive – and loll about on the beach until lack of money
pushed me back on to the same treadmill. I was never able to
balance work and play – it was either all one or all the other.

In addition to the nagging inner-child syndrome, this pattern is
also a part of not trusting one's animus or male energy, which we

use to accomplish everything in life. It is active, assertive, outgoing, whereas the anima or feminine energy is receptive and in-going. If we do not trust the inner male, we can become hard-working perfectionists, trying to compensate for our inadequacy, or start-stop people who never complete what they begin. Mistrust of the inner woman usually results in people cut off from, or denying the value of, feelings, imagination and intuition.

In my case I then did something that shocked me out of this pattern. I was writing a three-days-a-week page for a newspaper. I had carte blanche to write on any subject that came into my head. This was tremendously exciting and terrifying. I had two secretaries to whom I was meant to dictate my copy. I found I could not dictate without writing my ideas down first, so I stayed up most of the night working out what to dictate the following day. I worked seven days a week all day and half the night, in terror of failure.

Six months later my totally unrecognised inner child said: 'I've had enough of this!' and threw a tantrum. I found myself in the editor's office handing in my resignation. At home, I went into complete shock at what I had done. I felt as if I'd almost been possessed by another personality. For days, I sat and thought about my life, and suddenly a little voice in my head said: 'How old is the child in you now?' The number six popped up, and, closing my eyes, I saw in my imagination myself at six, curled up in a heap on a lawn, quivering with fear and apprehension, having been deposited in a boarding school with no explanation.

I felt the person I was at that moment merge with this little girl from the past, and I cried all the tears I was too afraid to cry on the lawn. I then imagined taking this child in my arms and talking to her. I told her I was very sorry that I had never before explained how much I loved her, that she was part of me and my life, and that we would spend lots of time together. We would play and have fun, meet people, travel, explore, learn, grow, and share things with each other.

Visualisations for the inner child

I stressed that I was *always* available to her, and that she could say anything to me, whether she was happy or sad, what she liked or disliked, and I would do the same with her. I imagined running outside with her on to a beautiful sunny beach. We splashed in the sea, collected shells, drew pictures in the sand, hurled sticks in the air for passing dogs to catch. I visualised our wandering through overgrown gardens, smelling the flowers, rolling in the grass, climbing trees, paddling in pools and streams, playing with kittens, ducks, ponies and puppies. I left her sitting on a swing with a kitten in one hand and a puppy in the other, and opened my eyes to find myself back in the present.

During the following days I did this visualisation exercise many times. I often began by asking myself, 'How old is the child in me today?' As the six-year-old healed the numbers changed, to eight or three or fourteen. Often a forgotten memory of something that had happened during one of these years would also pop us. As I dealt with each incident and fed this child in her inner reality, she stopped demanding attention from me in mine. I suddenly realised that I could not only heal the child by giving her the love and assurance she felt she had missed out on, but I could also heal the past, by using my imagination to recreate what had really happened. I saw that my past influenced me but should not control me. And so it is for all of us.

Using the power of imagination and fantasy – the Greek word *phantasia* means to make visible the invisible – we can explore every facet of ourselves, delve into our pain, our fears, phobias and traumas, and recreate our past, just as the editor of a book, film or play cuts out what does not work. The old age said that emotional healing was a life-long process which required a well-trained counsellor. The Quantum age, while not dismissing the well-trained counsellor, says that instant change, in all areas of our lives, from health to relationships to self-image, is possible, the magic wand being the power of the mind and imagination, through which we can work miracles.

There are dozens of different ways of getting in touch with and healing the inner child. Among those I have found the most successful are the following.

Visualisation I: Meeting your inner child

Close your eyes and imagine yourself walking through trees into a glade, where you will find your inner child. This child may appear as male or female, baby or adolescent, obedient or rebellious, sad or happy. Before speaking, take a moment to assess what you see, how you feel, what the child thinks and feels about him or herself, life, and you. Decide what this child most needs from you to be healthy and happy, and give it in abundance. Do not forget to give love, approval, support and reassurance, as well as asking forgiveness for not having done so before.

This type of exercise can free us from much of what is unconscious imprisonment to the past. You may want to substitute a room in a house for that glade, or imagine removing from the child's shoulders bricks that symbolise the weights of suffering unwillingly borne. The key to success in inner work, whether it be to heal the child, find the shadow or communicate with angels and guides, is to let the imagination play, and see what happens. Whether through visions, symbols, words or colours we are always shown exactly what we need to see.

Visualisation II: Your outer and inner self

Another simple but effective exercise is to imagine walking into a room where you also find a child. You notice it, but walk past it, through a door into another room, where you find a second child. Take time to compare the second child with the first. Is it older or younger, male or female, shy and withdrawn or smiling and happy? Most important of all, how does this second child respond to your presence? If you smile and hold out your hand, does it smile too, or shrink back in fear? The first child symbolises our outer self, the second the inner or hidden personality. At different times in our lives one or the other will appear dominant.

There is no right or wrong, better or worse in this exercise. It is simply a way of discovering whether your inner or outer self in the moment is the most happy and free. Having seen and compared the two, which often releases a great deal of repressed emotion, we must sense their reaction to each other, reassure and love them before taking them out of the house and releasing them to play together in the sun. When you do this you strengthen both inner and outer aspects of personality.

Extending visualisation

Visualisation exercises such as these can be used to change and heal almost any aspect of our lives, especially things we may dislike or fear to do. By involving our inner senses we radically sharpen our perceptions and powers in the outer world. To lose weight, win a race, climb a mountain or pass a test, see yourself doing it first in your mind's eye. The more you practise, the easier you will find it is to do whatever it is that you want to do.

A friend of mine who was a ballet dancer fell in love with, and subsequently married, a circus trapeze artist. Not wanting to live the kind of life where their work kept them apart, she decided to partner him on the trapeze. Very frightened of heights, she found the initial training almost impossible, until she began to use visualisation as part of the training. Three times a day she closed her eyes and imagined herself balanced on the high wire, performing incredible acrobatics with ease. She flew through the air from wire to wire, hung by her teeth and juggled balls as she pirouetted on the wire. To her amazement, this inner practice motivated her finally to climb the ladder up to the real wires in the circus tent, and begin her training in earnest. She said: 'I was still afraid, but something inside impelled me to feel the fear and do it anyway.'

No actor would dream of performing on stage without having rehearsed his part many times. Dreams, guided fantasies and reveries, in which we actively use our imagination, enable us all to rehearse as often as we like whatever parts we want to play next. We should remember that all such exercises work better if we relax the body first, by methods such as breath control or by tensing, then relaxing each muscle one by one from top to toe. A third way is to visualise light or colour washing through every part of our body.

In workshops in which I use guided imagery to help people

face and explore many aspects of themselves (both from this and other lives), I use all three methods as part of an overall preparation which deepens the experience.

Visualisation downwards and upwards

I have also found it helps, when exploring the unconscious and subconscious, to imagine going down rather than up. This can be done in various ways too. We can count backwards from twenty-one to zero, descend a flight of stairs or steps, float down a hill, a slope, a rainbow, or even imagine stepping on an escalator or taking a lift. The downward descent may lead into a cave, dungeon or cellar, but it is useful imagery if we want to find and heal our unconscious blocks, our shadow or subpersonality selves. We may not know what lies buried or hidden, but the willingness to go down into the depths can put us in touch with, and release, an energy that may present a hiccup in our lives today.

To explore higher levels of consciousness, to communicate with angels, teachers and guides, to align ourselves with our higher or overviewing soul selves, read our own Akashic records, or find our Book of Life, we should go up rather than down. To do this, we should imagine lifting the life force out of our bodies from toe to top, concentrating on each part from feet through ankles, calves, shins, knees, pelvis, chest, shoulders, neck, to the head and everything in-between, as if there were a magnet at the top of our skull that drew our energy up. We can imagine this energy or force like a balloon no longer tied to our physical body, but free to drift and float. We can see it lifting higher and higher, up and up into other realms of consciousness where we may find and speak with healers, teachers and guides who can give us insight into ourselves.

Moving into and out of a visualisation

Because some of us find visualisation difficult, especially when we begin, it is better if we create a backdrop for these meetings, by imagining an ancient temple or library, a special room or even a cave, where we can picture ourselves taking the hand of our mentor or guide, rather than try to force a clear picture. We

169

must not be afraid to ask questions, even if the only image we have is of yellow or brown or green spots before our eyes, instead of a sense of someone being there. Our intent to communicate with what is really our own inner wisdom always brings results.

However, instead of 'flashing lights in the sky' as answers to what we are desperate to know, the replies may pop up through the books we read, the radios we switch on, or the conversations we overhear while travelling to work. Some of us intuitively sense things rather than clairvoyantly see them. These can include words, symbols, shapes, colours and numbers, as well as people we have known or never seen before. To learn the language of both the inner and the higher self is similar to learning the language of dreams. It requires, like learning any other language, practice, humour and perseverance.

We should also remember that, however enjoyable it may be to float off into a different reality, and even if we want to stay there, we must bring ourselves back to the physical body before opening our eyes.

To do this, all we need is to reverse the imagery, float down rather than up. We can simply imagine the same bubble or balloon of consciousness or life-force drifting slowly and easily down until it rests on the top of our heads, when we can absorb it back into our bodies. We can then breathe it into the face, head and shoulders, into and through every cell, muscle, tissue and organ until we feel it anchored in our feet, and follow this by sighing, stretching, and pressing our feet to the floor until we feel ready to open our eyes. If we do not take the time and trouble to do this, we can feel disorientated and light-headed.

11

FREEDOM FROM PAIN AND FEAR

Journal writing

Another more external way of delving into our past in order to
face our future is through journal writing. Initiates in the
schools of Ancient Wisdom, the schools of esoteric learning,
sometimes known as Mystery Schools, learned how to move
freely between past, present and future, visible and invisible
realms, by using their imagination. Many of the visualisation
techniques we use today have come down to us from these
ancient schools. These are now available to all of us, instead of
just to the select few, and can help us to transform our lives.

The goal of the student in a mystery school was spiritual
growth, development of the personality, and perfection of the
character. Aside from inner work, each student was required to
keep a journal, recording the day's events, his reaction to them,
the effect of his prayers and the quality of his meditations.
Journal writing was a form of spiritual book-keeping, a means
of self-discovery and understanding, a map of the soul's journey
through life.

We can echo these teachings ourselves. To keep a journal in
which we record our dreams, note the people and qualities they
represent, the key events or situations with the most impact, our

emotional reactions to all this, combined with our daily thoughts and perceptions, will bring insight to the surface of our waking minds that we may not have recognised before. To do this, note: 'Where am I now?' as if writing the title of a chapter in a book. 'How long have I been in this phase? What happened to put me there?'

For example, my child died, my husband or wife left home, I read a book or lost my job. It may be very simple or very dramatic. We can use journal writing to go back through our lives from now to birth, the best and worst moments, what was working for and against us, the people, good or bad, and their effect on our lives, our ideals, hopes, fears, dreams and recollections which, as we look back, influenced us in some way.

I began recording my dreams and thoughts when I was six years old. I could pour words into my diary as if into the ears of an intimate friend who was totally receptive to anything I said or did. As an adult, I found that the combination of inner work with journal writing brought my inner and outer life together, so that the outer confirmed the inner and vice versa. This synthesis helped me to interpret, not just my past, but also the daily life events that unfolded around me.

The result was that every waking hour was filled with excitement and curiosity. Paul Solomon gave some of the best journal workshops I have ever attended. He suggested that we divided our journal into seven sections. The first dealt with the past. The second was like a daily log. The third noted the cast of characters that appeared in our day, what they did and how we reacted to them. The fourth was a letter to our higher self or inner teacher. The fifth was to record our dreams. The sixth was to describe the day's lessons or challenges and our attitude to them. The seventh section was to note any insights or inspirational thoughts that came up during our meditation.

These seven sections also relate to the seven chakras or energy points of the body. The key to success with Paul's formula was not to write too much. Some people find it easier to draw pictures and symbols in their journals instead of writing.

Mapping out your early childhood

In workshops, I sometimes use the following technique to
show the participants how best to understand the influences of
their early childhoods. I ask them to draw a circle and put
their name in the middle, and to write the names around the
edge of everyone who played a role in their first seven years.
By this, I mean those who were physically present, not Uncle
Charlie or a twice-removed cousin who lived in Timbuktoo,
who were part of the family but never seen. I then get the
seminar members to draw straight lines from their name to the
name of everyone who nurtured them – in the sense of
changing their nappies, feeding and burping them, and wiping
their noses.

They then draw wavy lines to those they felt comfortable and
happy with, and jagged lines to those with whom they felt ill at
ease and wary. It is possible to have both types of lines going to
the same person. I then suggest that the participants close their
eyes and ask themselves: 'Who really loved me, exactly as I was,
not because I made my bed, did my homework, or cut the grass
or did the washing-up.

The answers can shock. John, in a workshop, realised that an
old man he used to visit every day on his way home from school
was the only person in his childhood who gave him total and
unconditional acceptance, love and approval. He used to sit on
the old man's knee, while they read books, looked at birds' eggs,
and pored through old stamp albums together. One day his
parents came to collect him, and leapt to the conclusion that
their son was being molested. They dragged John off the old
man's knee and, shouting abuse, threatened to call the police.
John, aged seven, did not understand what the fuss was about.
His parents gave him no further explanation, and forbade John
ever to visit his friend again.

During this exercise John suddenly realised that a part of him
had frozen inside from that moment, and he wept. He also
recognised that, despite feeling unloved by his parents, they did
in fact love him, but did not show it. John healed his frozen
inner child over a period of time through writing letters to the

child of his past. He subsequently became a counsellor, special-
ising in children's problems.

Writing and drawing are powerful therapeutic tools, and can
provide immediate cathartic relief. By emptying our feelings on
to paper, we free ourselves of our pain and fear. We literally
write or draw them out of our system.

Forgiveness

When we reflect on the past, no matter how we go about it, we
often remember people we need to forgive. In fact, unwillingness
to forgive, or to let go of old memories, is, like lack of self-love,
one of the major blocks to happiness and success. During my
adolescence, it suddenly occurred to me that the divine in me
was able to do a lot that the 'poor little me' could not. I made up
a number of affirmations that I used to repeat in my head when
I felt insecure or unhappy. One of them was: 'I can, and will,
through God. God can and will through me.'

I had a lot of forgiving to do too, so when my rage or frustration made it virtually impossible for me to forgive, I would
imagine facing my then tormentor or oppressor, and saying to
them, my teeth often clenched, 'Through the divine in me, I
forgive the human in you and in me, which has caused this
problem.' Usually I did not feel an immediate wave of forgiveness flowing from me to the other person, but, on some level,
and within a few days, it always worked. The barriers between
us melted and we became friends again.

When we invoke the divine, in both ourselves and others, we
reach up to the highest levels in ourselves, which is way beyond
the struggling personality that holds on so tightly and refuses to
let go.

As well as invoking the divine to help me to forgive, I used to
write letters to the angels of people I was having difficulties with
– 'Dear angel, of Tom, Dick or Mary, please help me deal with
this situation –' which I then went on to describe. At the end I
said 'Thank you' and signed off 'With love, from Soozi'. This
too always worked, as if it bypassed the unconscious resistance

of the outer personality and was heard instead by their true essence. I still use this method to solve communication problems today. However, now, before signing off, I add, 'Please give me the right words, the opportunity and the courage to say them.' I then burn the letter in a candle flame. This is a form of written prayer. I have found it always succeeds.

Because I did this for years, I believed and felt that I had forgiven everyone in my life, including those who I felt had harmed me most. As I see it, true forgiveness, both of ourselves and others, means that we erase the memory of what happened so completely that it is as if it happened to someone else. In other words, 'the person I was, or they were then (whether from this or other lives), is not who I am or they are today.' We both have a different understanding and perspective, rather like an adult looking back at the child he was.

I later discovered that I had *not* in fact forgiven one particular person who was part of my painful childhood, although I had even believed that the karma was completed between us. In fact, when I heard the karmic chord between us snap, I collapsed on the floor with laughter. Soon afterwards I flew to Australia. On the way I became so ill that the immigration authorities assumed I had contracted a major infectious disease. Reluctant to let me into the country, they put me into quarantine for several days.

During this time I had a crisis similar to an NDE, or Near Death Experience, in which I found myself out of my body in what seemed to be an astral level. It was very dark, noisy and uncomfortable. Shadowy shapes brushed past me like cobwebs. I was very aware of the separation between myself and my body. I thought that if anyone found me like this they would think I was in a catatonic trance or had gone crazy, and would lock me up in a padded cell. Shivering and shaking, I thought I had gone crazy myself. Suddenly a figure appeared in front of me and said: 'Are you going to forgive X?'

Amazed, I replied: 'I have!' Three times I was asked the same question. Three times I replied that I had forgiven X. Suddenly I felt as if I had been struck on the head by an axe. I was cleft in half to the groin, where I discovered a raw bleeding wound, which was the accumulated pain of no love or support, and of childhood abandonment. I realised that I had forgiven X as much as I humanly could, but there was a residue. I began to weep and wail, to the extent of wanting to bang my head against the wall. Finally, and in fact three days later, this figure reappeared, and asked: 'Well, *are* you going to forgive X?' To my surprise, I heard myself saying that I wanted to, had tried to, but simply could not. This figure recoiled and, pointing a finger at me, said very sternly: 'I see. And you would condemn this entity to walk an astral level for eternity, yes?'

I realised at once that what he meant was the astral level similar to what some call purgatory. I was stunned. I had never realised that lack of forgiveness could put people in this terrible place. I thought of Hitler, and decided that I could not even condemn him to this purgatory, especially for eternity. 'Who am I?' I asked myself, 'to judge what anyone else does? It's all I can do to keep one foot after the other in dealing with my own life.' As these thoughts flew through my mind, I heard great sighs and groans fill the space around me. The ghostlike figures surrounding me tried to grab me, begging for help and release. They were desperate to live a physical life again and put right what they and others had done wrong.

However compassionate I felt, I could do nothing for them. I had the sensation of falling into and merging with my wound, and coming through it back into my body. Only then was I able totally to forgive X, with whom my relationship instantly changed. My understanding of forgiveness also changed. I realised that our refusal or resistance, both conscious and unconscious, to forgive, condemned not only others but also ourselves to this waste land. Many of us lose years, even many lives, chained to people we fear, hate and despise, while others are desperate to have the opportunity we have to be here on Earth now.

Forgiveness has always been a major factor in spiritual growth. As the consciousness of the planet lifts to another level, it is even more important than ever before. Our refusal to let go of the past literally chains us to it. We may think it easier to forgive once we are out of the physical body through death, and into another dimension, but, from all the descriptions of Near Death Experiences, this does not appear to be true. We get stuck with the very person we wanted to escape from, until we finally work through the problem. Aside from invoking the divine in us to forgive when the personality seems unable to, I have found the following exercise helpful.

Visualisation for cutting the cords

I close my eyes, and imagine following a path to a door, on the other side of which I am going to find the person I need or want to forgive. This may include my asking them for forgiveness too. I take a moment or two to reflect on what happened and how I reacted to it. How did I change and grow as a result of this experience? I open the door, and imagine the person in front of me. I first say exactly what I felt at the time, or what maybe I still feel now. It may include words of hate or despair.

Having got that off my chest, I take a few deep breaths, and look at the positive side. For example, my husband runs off with another woman and, after the initial shock and pain, I begin a new life which forces me to stand on my own two feet. I develop a strength and independence, an inner security which maybe I never had before. I then thank the person who was the catalyst for this, and ask to be shown the karmic bonds between us. These may appear in my mind's eye as thick ropes, bands of colour, silvery ribbons, threads or simply a sense of 'Yes, there's something there.'

I repeat my affirmation,

'Through the divine in me, I forgive the human in you and in me, and acknowledge the part you played in my life.' Using a sword, a knife, scissors or a candle-flame, or whatever else seems appropriate at the time, I cut through the cords. I mentally affirm: 'I cut these cords with the power of God.' When I sense that they are cut, I imagine my right hand on the navel of, first, the other person, and then of myself. I now say: 'I heal and seal this cord in the love of God.' I then release them to be what they truly are, and not who I want them to be. I imagine this person and myself surrounded by light, and, like an actor finishing a part in a play, therefore free to move on to something new. This is a particularly powerful method for changing and healing relationships with parents.

This does not mean that we sever all connection to them, but rather that we lift the relationship from the level of solar plexus to the heart. We then stop unconsciously pulling on one another. If we cut the cords in this way when strong emotional or sexual relationships came to an end, we would literally make a clean break and recover more easily. Relationships like these also create powerful psychic links which can stay with us long afterwards, leaving each of us vulnerable to the other. The type of exercise I have just described can also help us cut the cords that bind us to bad habits, past events, old memories of this and other lives, fears and apprehensions that continue to cause a hiccup in our progress today.

Fear of dying

All fears inhibit, but the fear of death is the greatest obstacle to living and the enjoyment of life. Western society conditions us to deny death as something catastrophic and unnatural. The process of dying is usually associated with fear, anxiety, and confusion. We fear pain and disease, of being incapacitated in some way, and therefore a liability to our families and friends. Fear of death includes the terror of letting go, of change, of the unknown, of leaving and losing everything that is loved and familiar. Many of us fear that we do not exist unless we are in a physical body, while others fear facing the consequences of what they have or have not done in life.

Selfishly, we dread the loss and loneliness caused by the death of someone we love. We usually whisper about death behind closed doors, as if it will go away like a bad dream if we refuse to acknowledge it. Yet we only have to look at nature to see that everything is constantly changing. Nothing is fixed, everything is impermanent. Nothing is born that does not die. A physical death is a spiritual birth, and the pangs of death a spiritual labour. By the same token, a physical birth is in a sense a spiritual death, a restriction of the consciousness we had before. Death and birth are neither a beginning nor an end, but part of the continuing cycle of creation. Each complements the other, and perhaps it takes confrontation with death to find the meaning of life.

Because I grew up with an awareness of other realities, and saw souls both in and out of the body, I had no fear of being physically dead. I believed, and still believe, in the continuity of life. Despite this, I had a great fear of the act of dying itself. I imagined that, no matter how we died, whether by accident, illness, violence or suicide, there would always be an unpleasant choking, a gasping for breath. I then had an NDE (Near Death Experience), which completely released me from this terror.

There was no sense of struggle. I found myself drawn through the top of my head out of my body and into a circle of white light, which was filled with a deep delphinium blue colour. Initially I felt as if I had popped out of clothes that were too tight. I had a sense of incredible expansion, freedom and excitement. I seemed to be floating, filled with peace and tranquillity. I remember thinking: 'If only people knew what it was like to die, they would not be so afraid.'

During this experience, I was shown that the only thing that really mattered in life, aside from living it to the full, was love; that lack of love, tolerance and kindness to one another was far worse than any major mistakes that we might consider that we had made. I saw that there were no mistakes. There were choices which led to different experiences, which would ultimately become part of our soul's wisdom and understanding.

I suddenly realised that I had expected judgement and punishment, but there was none, apart from how I judged and punished myself. I saw that at death we gain a wider perspective, but we do not immediately change consciousness as a result of no longer being in a physical body. I understood too that it was easier to deal with any 'unfinished business' *before* we died, rather than afterwards, and that we create our future astral or emotional body by the way we live today.

I had no sense of threat or coercion, but rather one of freedom and choice to do or be whatever I wanted. Drawn back into my body, I felt exhilarated as never before. I was free to explore, touch and taste everything life had to offer. Since then I have met and talked to hundreds of people across the world who have had similar experiences. Not only had they lost their fear of death and dying, so that they were more fully alive than ever before, but they also agreed that, in the words of Albert Schweitzer: 'The real tragedy of life is what dies inside a man while he lives.'

Khalil Gibran wrote:

You would know the secret of death.
But how shall you find it unless you seek it in the heart of life?
The owl whose night-bound eyes are blind unto the day cannot
*   unveil the mystery of light.*
If you would indeed behold the spirit of death, open your heart
*   wide unto the body of life.*
For life and death are one, even as the river and the sea are
*   one.*

As this century comes to an end, and we move into the next millennium, it is more essential than ever before that we drop the old fears of death which limit, bind and blind us. Death is an initiation, a ritual or rite that allows us to expand beyond the limitation of the physical body.

In ancient esoteric schools, initiates were placed inside a sarcophagus for days at a time, during which they were expected to leave their bodies, explore astral and other realms, and then return and report to their teachers all that they saw and discovered. The current flood of Near Death Experiences seems to me to be a replacement of these initiations, and, though not total proof of life after death, does provide some evidence for it. I believe that these NDEs are partly preparing us for a future when we shall operate in a much lighter and more etheric body.

This new body will enable us to raise or lower our vibrations, rather as we might change gears in a car, in order to move between planes without suffering our present often traumatic physical birth and death. We shall learn what we need to learn, do what we need to do, then move on. We shall participate much more consciously in the transition we today call death. Many people are already doing this, that is, neatly packing up all their affairs when they feel their hour has come, then lying down to die quite unmelodramatically.

Sending light and love to the dying

We can help suicide victims by holding, in our mind's eye, an image of them surrounded by and filled with light. Even if we do not understand why they killed themselves, we can help to release them from this grey fog by giving them love and reassurance, and reminding them of our happy times with them. No matter how people die, they all need love, light and blessings. We must also remember that we shall meet again all those whom we have truly loved.

The power of love to heal, transform and change anything in life is limitless. Elizabeth Kubler Ross, who specialises in death and dying, decided to open her house in Virginia to babies born with Aids. Most of their mothers were prostitutes who also had Aids. Fearful of the consequences when their babies were born, they had abandoned them in doorways or on hospital steps. Kubler Ross was prevented from using her house in this way by local people who feared that she was bringing Aids into the community. Instead, a number of volunteer families took the babies into their own homes for what was presumed would be only a few months until they died. They gave them so much love that they literally loved the babies back to life. Many recovered from the virus and were pronounced completely healthy.

If we ourselves loved our bodies when ill, instead of rejecting them and treating them like an enemy, we would recover more easily. Illness is a message, a communication from the soul. It is a confrontation in the physical of what we are reluctant to deal with mentally or emotionally, and thus a unique opportunity for transformation. However, we also need to remember that ultimate healing is release from the physical body: there is a time to be born and a time to die. No death happens by accident, however we see it from our limited human perspective.

When Plato was on his death-bed, he was asked the key to life. 'Prepare for death,' he replied. We can prepare for death the same way as we prepare for a birth. Simple breathing, relaxation and meditational exercises, together with a periodic review of life, and working on whatever needs to be put right, are all good preparations. We can also use dreams, visualisation, and writing.

Visualising your own death

For example, I can use dreams and visualisation to imagine myself dying easily. It is like a dress rehearsal for the real thing. I could also ask to be shown how I died in another life. If I have a fear of the manner in which I die, such as lying paralysed for months on end after a heart attack, a good way to deal with it is to write as full a description as possible of what this would be like for myself and for my family; how would I feel, and what would I physically experience, and think? I would then burn it. I next describe how I would choose to die, in as much detail as possible. I do not burn this, but tuck it away in a drawer or in my journal. From time to time I re-read it, and sometimes visualise myself dying in the way I have chosen. This ritual, however simple, helps to programme my mind for a happier death.

The more we practise meditation and visualisation and our expansion of consciousness beyond the physical reality which they present, the easier it will be for us to move on. We can help one another make this transition by creating an atmosphere of peace and light around a dying person, instead of the doom, gloom and despondency usual in such cases. Crystals, flowers, candles, sandalwood, soft music, fragrant-smelling herbs, or oils to give a light massage, all help us move our consciousness into the spiritual dimension.

A friend of mine sings to her dying patients, and will often hold them in her arms as they take their last breath. Another friend, a nurse, gently massages their feet and hands, and tells them it is all right for them to go – all they need to do is to follow the light and stay with it until they see a familiar face. Myrtle, a friend who died of cancer two years ago, was taken by her husband Jack to the hospice only hours before her death. He sat and stroked her hair, and spoke soothingly to her about their life together, even though she was barely conscious. Suddenly, to the surprise of another friend who was also in the room, Jack pulled back the covers and got into bed with Myrtle. For about an hour he held her lovingly, telling her gently it was all right for her to leave him. With a tiny sigh, she died.

Tragically, most of us die desperately alone and uncomforted in a hospital bed, although invisible spiritual help is always present. Future generations will judge our current attitude to death and dying as completely barbaric. However, by then humanity will almost certainly no longer fear death, but see it as an ever-present part of the process of life. In the past, ancient peoples saw sleep as a little death, and death as a little sleep. The Essenes prepared for death every night, by leaving nothing undone or unfinished that they might regret if they did not awake the next day. They greeted each morning as if it were the start of a new life.

If enough of us today could also see death as a little sleep, and that we die in order to become new, we could help humanity rid itself of this needless dread. Our minds and imaginations, when joined with hundreds of others, have the energy and power to create deep and lasting change in the world. What happens is what is called critical mass, when a certain number of individuals affect the consciousness of all others.

Death is a metamorphosis – the caterpillar turning into the butterfly. Dying is the process of discarding an outer sheath, like an old coat that imprisons the essence of who we are. Death is freedom from restriction. In the words of Goethe:

'Nature invented death that there might be more abundant life ... If you have not got this, this concept of death and becoming, you are but a dull guest in a dark world.'

12

INTO THE NEXT
MILLENNIUM

. . . We are in a time so strange
That living equals dreaming,
And this teaches me that man
Dreams his life, awake.

CALDERON, *La Vida es Sueño*

Nostradamus's predictions for the end of the millennium

A French doctor who lived in Provence over 400 years ago predicted these 'times so strange' in detail. Nostradamus was his name. Nostradamus was probably one of the greatest mystics and prophets ever known to mankind. In the 1500s he predicted that the end of the millennium would be charged with conflicts and upheavals, earthquakes, global warming, famine, flood, holes in the ozone layer, black holes, spacecraft crashes, and Aids sweeping the Earth 'like a plague of locusts'. Long before their invention he foresaw cars, aeroplanes, television, radio, weapons of war, industrial machines, and much of the modern technology we take for granted today. He predicted the use of sound waves to kill cancer, new treatment for old age and senility, and how genetic science would discover the cause of disease rather than merely use drugs to treat its symptoms.

Nostradamus burned all his papers before his death for two

reasons. First, he did not want them to fall into the wrong hands. Second, he did not want to frighten the people around him, for the changes he predicted were far more rapid and cataclysmic than anything that had happened in the world before. He then condensed his original prophecies into obscure verses known as quatrains, to prevent future generations also from knowing too much about the changes to come. His predictions cover thousands of years, but their main thrust seemed always the 1990s and the new epoch.

Our impending evolution

I am quite sure that a man of Nostradamus's time who suddenly found himself in the twentieth century would indeed think that 'living equals dreaming', as we might if we could see into the future a few hundred years from now. I have previously described the changes that lie ahead as being as great as when man first came out of the water and walked on land. Perhaps this was more true of the Renaissance man than any other. Today, instead of moving from water to land, we are moving from the Earth into the sky, to inter-planetary exploration and colonisation.

To do this we need to adapt. To survive underwater we need diving equipment. When we step out of the water our wet suits, flippers, goggles and air tanks hinder rather than help us. We remove them quickly. I believe that in a few hundred years man will no longer have the physical body he has today. However amazing and wonderful our bodies may be today, they may be too dense for the new world to which we are even now adapting.

Many years ago, during a workshop on male-female relationships, I had a dream in which I saw what the dream described as the sons and daughters of God coming to Earth for the first time. They were sparks of light encased in etheric bodies who came down to the Earth to play. Initially androgynous, these sons and daughters of God projected parts of themselves into rocks, trees, flowers, even animals, to discover what it felt like. Many of them got stuck and forgot their origins, and thus became trapped in matter.

We, their descendants, who also came to Earth to find out what it was like to be spirit encased in matter are now, with planet Earth herself, lifting from matter into spirit. I believe that our future bodies will be light, etheric, and have the same power of projection. Our minds will be clear, light and open. We shall no longer fear death, hunger and thirst, cold or heat. Instead of driving cars or flying in aeroplanes, we shall simply move about the globe by projecting our consciousness to wherever we want to go. Tibetan lamas, Indian sages, medicine men and women from various indigenous tribes have always done this.

The desire to be in a certain place, or spend time with a particular friend, will automatically draw us to them. If we want to know what is happening anywhere in the world, or even on other planets, we shall 'switch on' clairvoyantly and telepathically, exactly as we switch on the radio or television today. Reincarnation, past-life therapy, and the laws of karma or cause and effect, will be accepted not just as a theory, but as a fundamental requirement for self-understanding.

Future education and communication

Our current process of reasoning will appear formal and dead. Intuition and creative imagination will be more important than logic and intelligence. Even today, education is no longer an automatic guarantee of work. The widespread use of computers and advanced technology have already introduced us to the idea that new generations are evolving who will never work in the same way as man did in the past. Ultimately this will dissolve the barriers between the right and the left brain, and push us to identify ourselves with who we are, rather than what we do.

Future children, instead of lessons of reading, writing and arithmetic, will learn how universal laws, such as the Kabbalah, can be applied to any aspect of life, from running an office to building a house. Instead of the current dry, text-book studies of history, children will be shown how to read the Akashic record, and even how to project themselves into past historical events. Their education will include a review of their own past lives, in order that they see and understand the dominant tendencies in them, and correct those felt to be destructive.

They will not be segregated as now by age, but rather by interest. Classes are more likely to take place in gardens and parks, rather than in institutionalised buildings as at present. Students will be encouraged to study the heavens, the sun, the phases of the moon, the movements of the planets, as well as astrology, numerology, palmistry and phrenology. Instead of suffering written exams, they will be guided by astrological and numerological charts to discover the issues or concerns that affect or interest them.

Schools of the future will teach their pupils how to develop their psychic powers and occult wisdom. They will learn how to read the omens, portents and symbols presented in the shifting shapes of clouds, the movement of the wind, the flutter of a butterfly's wing, the patterns in the sand, a feather on the ground, as much as by their study of the occult sciences such as the Tarot.

The Tarot cards come from the occult schools of ancient Egypt. Originally designed to help students learn how to decipher the hieroglyphs which depicted the mysteries of life and death, and how best to adapt to them, they have now become for many a symbol of fortune-telling. When used properly and with reverence, they can be a key for exploration of our sub and unconscious selves. Much of the new teaching will come from discarnate entities, angels and guides.

In Nostradamus's time, this type of communication was called prophecy. In Edgar Cayce's, it was described as a reading. Today we call it channelling. All over the world there are currently hundreds of people claiming to be channels for discarnate entities. These range from your uncle, who died last year – and, however willing to help, no wiser than when he was incarnate – to beings of incredible intelligence and understanding such as Seth, channelled by the late Jane Roberts, who inspired thousands of people internationally to see themselves and life in a different way.

Many others claim connection to star people from the Pleiades or Venus. I believe that the current explosion of channelling is indicative of the dissolving barrier between physical and spiritual worlds. In future 'channelling' will be accepted as completely normal, and invisible teachers as common as university professors.

People of the future will use telepathy and clairvoyance as their means of communication. They will have new accelerated forms of learning, which will include conscious changing of the brain-wave rhythm. Instead of morning prayers, or commands to pay attention, tomorrow's children will probably be guided into a state of deep meditation which will help them absorb information more easily.

Years ago Jose Silva, founder of Silva Mind Control, guided the extremely poor Mexican children he was trying to teach into an altered state of consciousness before he began the day. Because many of them arrived at the school barefoot and hungry, he also got them to imagine eating a large breakfast. Almost immediately, his pupils began to learn better, and even developed a psychic sensitivity which enabled them to know what he was going to say before he said it. His success led him to develop the techniques presented under the title of Silva Mind Control.

Children will be encouraged to seek for knowledge within themselves, rather than just from a teacher, a book, a video or computer. They will refer to intuition for guidance, rather than an outside authority, and learn the language of dreams as naturally as we learn French or German. They will also learn that it is not knowledge that builds the soul, but rather its application to daily life. Their education will draw out of them exactly what they need to fulfil their potential instead of stifling it as much of our education does today.

A very sad example of this is the story of a child in Canada who loved to draw the sun, the sky and vast landscapes with no horizon. His teacher urged him to 'draw planes, trains, cars and houses like Johnny does'. At twelve he committed suicide, after writing a verse to his teacher in which he said he lost all his joy from having to sit at a square desk in a square room, in a square building surrounded by a square playground, draw and write on neat little squares of paper and copy what everyone else did. In the future, children will be encouraged to explore the heights and depths of creation, and freely to express their own individuality. By then, they will probably be androgynous, but will also know that they have occupied both male and female bodies, that neither is superior to the other, but simply offers a different opportunity and experience.

Contacting your guide through meditation

While children of the future may instinctively know how to contact their teachers and guides, how do we go about it today? The answer is meditation. Meditation bypasses the conscious mind and opens us to infinite wisdom and the reality of God and other realms. We are already channellers or mediators for the energy that, in moving through us, enables us to accomplish what we need to do. However, most of us do this unconsciously. To make a conscious connection with a teacher, guide or wisdom beyond our human perception, it is best to prepare a little.

Aside from the breathing and relaxation techniques I described previously, we should wash, and then put on, either in reality or imagination, a garment that signifies the importance of what we are about to do. This will impress on mind, body and spirit that we are about to enter another dimension. We can make this effect all the more realistic if we also imaginatively create a special or sacred place, such as a mountain cave, an island, a temple or a forest glade – whatever may be most meaningful to us in the moment. We should now, with eyes closed, visualise our teacher or guide appearing in front of us, and say to him or her: 'Please, I want to get to know you better. I want to see you, feel you, hear you. I want to know that you are near me, participating in my life.'

Listen to the reply and write it down. Initially we may feel that we are making it up. I know that I thought this myself when, after months of meditation, words poured into my mind which I had no option but to write down. I felt slightly ashamed and even crazy, thinking that this was

---

perhaps the only way in which my subconscious could express itself. Finally, I showed a friend some of the information that 'came through' in this way, and asked if she thought it nonsensical. She roared with laughter, and told me it was far too intelligent for me to have made it up. I began to trust this superior intelligence, but I also questioned it, and asked for proof that this information came from beyond me, rather than from me.

Not knowing just what proof to ask for, I said: 'Speak to me like Noël Coward, Samuel Johnson, Thomas Mann, Charles Dickens, Somerset Maugham . . .' The words and language changed instantly, reflecting each writer in a way that I could never have done. This proof was also given to me independently in many forms. For example, a string of words spoken by my guide which I had written down would be repeated to me verbatim by a stranger on a bus, or an astrologer who unexpectedly offered to read my chart. Since then, this guidance has been one of the main factors which has helped me to live my life in a totally different way.

Many people may think it wrong to question what appears to be a deeply spiritual experience, but I believe we should always question its validity. Ultimately, we must learn to trust ourselves, our own authority, develop our own integrity and completeness of being, without dependence on anything or anyone else – whether incarnate or discarnate.

To channel is to listen, to allow something to come through, rather than to push or force something to happen. Our guides may appear in a non-physical form, such as lines of light or colour. For a long time I saw my own guides as little round smiley faces, or yellow boxes each with 'love' written on them, or sometimes hearts cascading out of the ceiling. There is no need to try to force images. It is, rather, better to imagine what it would feel like to be in the presence of a beloved older brother or sister who knew everything about you, completely loved and accepted you, and could advise you on any aspect of life you chose to ask about.

Visualising your Book of Life

It is sometimes helpful to ask your guide for your Book of Life, as a trigger to opening your consciousness to this type of communication. Imagine the colour, size and weight of such a book. In your mind's eye see your name embossed on the cover, feel the paper, thick or thin, leather-bound or not, old or new.

The more you practise this type of exercise, the clearer your answers will be. When you open it, what does its text say? You may not see exact words, but allow whatever impressions emerge to flow into your mind, and write them down. Always remember to say thank you to your guide. The book *God Calling* was written in this way, as were many other books that inspire and help us.

Children of the next millennium will, in their new light bodies, see auras as clearly as we see the physical body today. Knowing that whatever they think and feel will be instantly revealed in the auric field, their education will include aura-cleansing and chakra-balancing.

The chakras

The chakras are seven vital centres that go from the top of the head to the base of the spine. They are like power points where lines of energy meet and cross. The chakras control the organs and glands of the body, and each one relates to a different frequency on the colour scale. The main chakras are:

1 The *root*, at the base of the spine. The related colour is red; the gland is the gonads.

2 The *spleen*, or *sacral* chakra, two to three inches below the navel. The related colour is orange; the gland is the adrenals.

3 The *solar plexus*, at the diaphragm. The related colour is yellow; the gland is the pancreas.

4 The *heart*, mid chest. The related colour is green, the gland is the thymus.

5 The *throat*. The related colour is blue; the gland is the thyroid.

6 The *brow*, or *third eye* in the centre of the forehead. The related colour is indigo; the gland is the pituitary.

7 The *crown* chakra, at the top of the head. The related colour is violet; the gland is the pineal.

There is another centre, whose colour is white, about eighteen inches above the crown, and others including in the knees and feet, but it is more usual to focus on the seven I have just described.

The seven major chakra points in our bodies mirror seven invisible inner planes. Our chakra balance or imbalance show how well (or not) we have mastered the qualities of each one. The chakras were originally associated with the Seven Planets of Saturn, Venus, Mars, Jupiter, Mercury, the Sun and the Moon. When Uranus, Neptune and Pluto were discovered, three more chakras were activated.

In addition, seven colour rays, or streams of energy, affect our physical, mental, emotional and spiritual make-up and influence our personalities. Although specific rays are ascribed to each chakra, there is no fixed pattern as all the rays, in turn, play through each of the seven major chakras. A ray analysis can help us understand the energies dominant in each one of us, while a chakra analysis indicates how we use these energies.

The First Ray is associated with will, power and authority. The challenge is to use power aligned with love and spiritual awareness rather than the ego. The Second Ray is one of love, wisdom and understanding. Spiritual teachers, school teachers, philosophers, intuitives or sensitives, are usually born on, or influenced by, this ray. The challenge for them is balancing intuition with intellect. The Third Ray is one of creativity. Inventors, designers of industry and business technology are associated with this ray's power to develop ideas and intelligence. Here, the challenge is to be tolerant of others who are not so quick to understand or respond to the new idea.

The Fourth Ray affects the emotional body and can cause over-sensitivity. The challenge here is to bring harmony and balance into areas of conflict. The Fifth Ray energises the mental body, and here the need is to integrate spiritual and mental knowledge. The Sixth Ray is one of devotion and people who are strongly affected by its energies can become fanatical. The challenge is not to judge everything as either perfect or perfectly intolerable but to see the value in all. The Seventh Ray is one of transformation and transmutation and people influenced by it tend to like ritual. This is fine as long as it does not cut us off from the physical world around us. Because we now begin to remember that we are multi-dimensional beings, we are all influenced by every Ray and are literally becoming Rainbow People.

To understand how our chakras influence our behaviour, I include a brief description of the qualities of each one, but suggest that, for a more detailed explanation, you read one of the many excellent chakra books available.

The Root or Base Chakra has to do with survival (fight or flight), sexuality, food and all aspects of Earthly life. This chakra is literally our anchor to the physical world. When balanced we accept life, death and birth. We believe the Earth is a secure and happy place and that all our physical needs, such as money, work, relationships etc., will be met. If this chakra is weak or imbalanced, we will either struggle to cope, feeling insecure and uncertain, or try to dominate and exploit the world around us. Other symptoms of imbalance on this level are an excessive focus on material possessions, sex, food, alcohol; an obsession with satisfying personal desires without thought of others (i.e. simple selfishness) or so much worry and anxiety we simply cannot function.

The Sacral or Spleen Chakra has to do with creativity and instinctive or gut-level reactive emotion. These energies allow us to flow and interact empathetically with others and, when in balance, we will do just that: if out of balance we may block our feelings and appear cold and unemotional or emotionally manipulative. We may also suffer sexual frustration, or sexual difficulties that lead into too much sex or fantasising about it. Blockages on this chakra level can also lead us into drug and alcohol addiction as well as sexual indifference.

The Solar Plexus Chakra is associated with communication, relationships, social identity, self-esteem, likes and dislikes. When this chakra is healthy we feel open to others, joyous, abundant, altruistic and self-accepting. If it is out of balance, we can suffer chronic lack of self-worth and inferiority. We may do things merely to conform or win approval as well as suffer chronic digestive problems.

The Heart Chakra is our link between the lower and higher chakras as well as between the visible and invisible. It is the level of unconditional love and acceptance and, when balanced, we love and feel loved; we will radiate love and happiness to others. When out of balance the energies of this chakra can stimulate jealousy, greed, a need for recognition for what we do or say, as well as a lack of flexibility which can make us possessive and too dependent on external people and situations.

The Throat Chakra, similar to the Solar Plexus, is also associated with communication but it is more the expression of our own truth, will and real identity. When the throat chakra is balanced we will express ourselves in a tone and manner that is easy to understand and comfortable to listen to. We will share thoughts and feelings fearlessly and also listen to others. When out of balance on this level, we may stutter, become totally silent or talk trivia, develop a lump in our throats or talk too much or too aggressively.

The Third Eye Chakra is associated with intuition, imagination and access to visible and invisible worlds. When balanced we have the abilities of clairvoyance, telepathy and intuitive guidance. If out of balance we jump into intellectual overload, i.e. we only accept what we see, taste, touch, feel and hear; and we see anything spiritual (such as books or discussion) as a complete waste of time. We may also try to force our opinions on others.

The Crown Chakra is a level of spiritual understanding and a merging of inner and outer, physical and material, visible and invisible worlds. This energy connects us to angels and guides; we can ask questions and receive answers. When out of balance on this level we may fear death and feel life is pointless and so escape into endless activity.

Assessing the health of the chakras

A simple way to assess the health or otherwise of the chakras is to imagine the body as a seven-storey building, and move from basement to roof assessing each floor as we go. On the roof, we can meet the caretaker, and ask if he or she thinks one floor needs more attention than another. A friend of mine who did this discovered that she had a problem when going up in a lift, when she could not get out at the fifth floor – equivalent to her throat. She suddenly realised that she never said what she really wanted to say, fearing how others might perceive her. When I did this exercise myself, I saw that the walls on the sixth floor were crumbling. I later discovered that I had osteo-arthritis in my jaw.

There are many ways to assess the balance or imbalance of our chakras. We can read chakra books and see which classification strikes a chord in us. We can use a pendulum, or rather get a friend to do so, and check them out. We can use imagination and visualisation, such as in the exercise I just described. We can use kinesiology or touch for health. I frequently use this method to test chakras in seminars or with friends. First, extend your left arm and let someone press down on the wrist, while you resist. This allows them to feel your normal muscle strength. (NB: 'resist' does not mean fight.) Then place your right hand on whatever chakra you choose (I usually go through them all) and again extend your left arm to be pressed. If the chakra is weak, your arm will weaken, if strong, your arm will lift up a little.

Recognise which chakras react to shock, stress or emotion. If our chakras are balanced, we won't react in the same way. For example, shock or stress might make us feel angry, out of control or even susceptible to diarrhoea, when it hits the root chakra. On a heart level, we may have a racing pulse or feel our heart skip a beat; shock reaction in the spleen area can make us overreact or stifle our feelings, while in the solar plexus we become queasy, helpless and nervous. Our throat chakra may react with an attack of choking, coughing and speechlessness. Our Third Eye reaction may be a headache or mental confusion, while the Crown Chakra may respond with lower backache.

The following exercises can all help to bring the chakras back into balance.

Balancing the chakras

The flow of energy between the chakras affects our physical health as well as our sense of well-being, so it is a good idea to take care of them. There are a number of ways to balance the chakras, including the use of crystals. One way is to take a four to five inch natural quartz crystal pressed firmly against the palm of your right hand, and hold it, point down, a few inches above each chakra, rotating it both clock- and anti-clockwise, depending on which chakra you are treating.

In a woman, the chakra is anti-clockwise at the crown, clockwise at the brow, anti-clockwise at the throat, clockwise at the heart, anti-clockwise at the solar plexus, clockwise at the spleen, and anti-clockwise at the root. In the man, it is the exact opposite. If you make an anti-clockwise movement on a chakra whose natural flow is clockwise, it can cause discomfort. If you hold a crystal on or near chakras, it can also balance them as well as recharge the aura. It does not matter whether you start at the crown or the base, and, although you can do it for yourself, it is more effective if another does it to you.

A good alternative way of balancing the chakras is to imagine white light pouring into each centre from the one above the top of the head. Sit on a chair with your spine straight, or lie down flat, and visualise the light coming through the skull and flowing to each chakra from crown to base. You can also visualise circles or stars of colour glowing on each chakra. When I do this, I prefer to go from base to crown. I find this extra powerful if I chant sound with each colour. As a child, I used to see everything around me as kaleidoscopic waves of sound and colour – music had colour, colour was music. To quote Christopher Hills, founding member of the University of the Trees in America, 'everything in creation is singing its own song'.

The sounds I use are ones I learnt from an amazing spiritual teacher, psychic and metaphysician called William David in America. William used to be an opera singer, and teaches all his students how to work with colour and sound, so that they can each find their own unique soul-song and join in with what is literally the music of the spheres. We chant these sounds of colour in all my workshops. They have a similar effect on our physical bodies, chakras, auras and states of consciousness as do crystals. The more we practise, the more effective they become. The correlation between these colours and sounds is:

● Pitch middle C for red
● Pitch B above middle C for blue
● Pitch E above middle C for yellow
● Pitch G above middle C for orange
● Pitch D above middle C for green
● Pitch A above middle C for indigo
● Pitch F above middle C for purple/violet.

A quick pick-me-up if we feel distressed by the traumas of these times is to sit in an orange bath – use a few drops of orange cake colouring or Aura-Soma – and sing 'EH' for twenty to thirty minutes, then wrap yourself up warmly and go to bed.

Colour therapy

Colour therapy is already widely used to treat many of today's problems. It can range from placing violent criminals or mental patients in pale pink rooms, to electro-crystal treatment which beams colour into specified areas of the diseased or ill body. I recently saw a computer image of a woman which showed a lot of red in her throat. After the treatment, it became blue, and therefore healthy for that area. In the ancient and now sunken city of Atlantis, the priests and priestesses clairvoyantly saw blocks in the energy system of a person, which indicated disease, which was then treated by colour, crystal lasers (also used in orthodox medicine today) and sound waves, that balanced the inner as well as the outer bodies.

In the world to come, people will probably have the ability to beam sound and colour waves into the ill or indisposed, without recourse to instruments. Meanwhile, we can all improve the quality of our health and our sense of well-being by visualising or wearing the colours we think most beneficial to us.

A colour meditation

A colour meditation I use both for myself and in workshops is to imagine entering different-coloured tents or rooms in a house. Sometimes I simply go into them and think of the colours renewing and revitalising all the organs, cells, muscles and tissues in my body. At other times I use the colours as a means of connection to different aspects of myself.

For example, I might imagine entering a red tent to find my animus or masculine side, a blue tent to find my anima or female side, orange to see who needs forgiveness, green to find my shadow, yellow to find not only the child of my past but also the pure inner divine child, indigo to look for past lives that may affect my life today, and violet to look for future or even co-existent selves. I finish with a white tent, in which I meet my teacher or dream guide, and ask for information or help, or else I simply imagine myself bathed with light before I open my eyes again.

To get the full benefit of this exercise, it may be better if you record it on a tape and listen to it later. We can visualise entering all the tents one after another in the same thirty to forty minutes, or take one tent a day. Either way, this exercise can bring a lot of insight.

In the 1960s Christopher Hills introduced the idea of creative conflict in which assessment of people by the colour of their personality helped bring about understanding. For example, the yellow intellectual must allow for the red level man to become impatient over meticulous and lengthy planning. The red personality man has to accept that the blue may seek an authority-basis for his decisions, while the yellow planner tries to fit everything into a logical framework. The orange person may base what he or she does on a sense of approval or disapproval from those around him or her.

Every soul comes into incarnation on one of seven rays, which Alice Bailey, the great Theosophist, described in detail in her many books. Each ray has a different vibration and colour, and produces a different psychological type. Christopher Hills's work is another way of looking at the same thing. Today we may assess what colour a person is from the way he or she behaves. The people of tomorrow will immediately understand another person's behaviour or attitude by seeing what ray they incarnated on, and the colours predominant in the aura.

Aura cleansing exercises

Auric colours can change, depending on what we are doing or how we are feeling. The more physical we are, the more dense the colours, the more spiritually awake, the lighter and more etheric the colours will be. Children of the future will cleanse their auras as automatically as the children of today clean their teeth. The following method is one I use myself every morning when I wake up and every night before I go to bed. If I feel at all wobbly during the day, I do it then too.

I shake my hands in front of me as if I were shaking off drops of water, and in doing so re-charge my electro-magnetic field. I put my forefingers and index fingers on my brow, then pull them down over my cheeks to under my jaw, and shake my hands off again. Next, I cup my hands under my chin, and lift my linked hands over the top of my head and down to the back of my neck, and shake my hands off in front of me again. I do this last complete movement three times.

I follow this by putting my right hand across to my left shoulder, then brushing down through my auric field to my feet, repeating the same with my left hand to my right shoulder, and down. Next, I put my hands behind me at the small of my back, and brush straight down to my heels, ending by bringing my hands low in front of me, and shaking them off. Finally, I cup my hands in front of my chest, then lift them over my head to the back of my neck, and bring them forward to brush down all the way to my toes, and shaking the crumbs of impurity off my hands to be transformed by God's light.

We can also practise radiating light or colour into the aura from the solar plexus as if we had swallowed the sun, in order to strengthen the aura. After this exercise, I always invoke the presence of the Archangels Michael, Gabriel, Uriel and Raphael for my support and protection, and seal off my aura by imagining myself within a five-pointed star.

Balancing your male and female sides

A visualisation exercise that I enjoy doing from time to time, which puts me in touch with how balanced or not my male and female sides are, is as follows: I make myself comfortable, take a few deep breaths and relax. With my eyes closed, I imagine the left side of my brain, the feel and colour of it, whether it is free and open or tight and restricted. The left brain is the logical or masculine side, the right brain the intuitive, imaginative or feminine side. The left brain controls the right side of the body, the right brain controls the left.

Thus, symbolically, the left is generally considered feminine, and the right masculine. I then visualise my right brain, and compare the two sides, which can sometimes appear to be very different. I am usually more comfortable in my right brain. In the same way, I now imagine the left and right halves of my body. I move from one to the other, and sense which in the moment is stronger or weaker.

I then imagine holding a symbol for my male energy in my right hand, and for my female in my left, and again sense which is stronger or weaker, lighter or heavier. I cup my hands, palms upwards, on my lap, and again compare the two before absorbing them into my solar plexus. I then flood my body from top to toe with either light or colour, blending and harmonising both left and right, male and female halves.

This exercise can not only help us to assess the predominance of male/female, and bring them into balance, but also helps to dissolve the barriers between left and right hemispheres of the brain. Another form of this exercise is to stare at your own face in a mirror, covering first the left side, then the right with an A4 sheet of paper. Next, you assess whether the left eye is more open or closed than the right, the eyebrow thicker, thinner, higher or lower, and examine the shape of the cheek, nostril, the droop of the mouth, and again compare left and right, and assess their balance. This is an interesting exercise to do with a partner, and also with the well-known faces of people such as politicians. Our faces symbolise our identities, and reveal how comfortable or uncomfortable we are with our masculine and feminine aspects.

Brain expansion exercise

To do this as a brain-expanding exercise, rather than an assessment of male and female, simply visualise different things happening in each hemisphere of the brain. For example, imagine nails scraping down a blackboard in the left, the sharp, sour taste of a freshly cut lemon in the right, the sound of the sea in the left, glass breaking in the right, a baby crying in the left, a woman screaming in the right, the fragrance of perfume or wild flowers in the left, the smell of freshly ground coffee or badly burnt toast in the right – or anything else that can vividly conjure up taste, sight or sound that stimulate both left and right hemispheres.

The coming spiritual age

Tomorrow's focus will be on spiritual rather than worldly developments. Most orthodox religions today separate man from God, and have deteriorated into meaningless sets of rules and regulations in which the original spirit of truth has become cloaked in dogma. These rules repress and punish impersonally, and control rather than uplift. True spirituality is light, expansive, humorous, not fearsome and restrictive. It is alive with love, laughter, joy, fun and celebration.

To understand the spirit of God, we have to open our hearts to a love beyond human comprehension. We can do this anywhere, and often more easily in the simple surroundings of a garden, a beach, or even our own beds at home, rather than within the cold stone walls of a church or temple. Religious rites were meant to free, not imprison us, and in the future will do just that, by reminding us of the sacred, and that the spirit world and this interact, that we are part of an intelligence that permeates the universe. In the words of Alexander Pope, we shall know 'All are but parts of one stupendous whole, whose body nature is, and God the soul.'

As the barriers dissolve between spirit and matter, as modern physics merges with ancient philosophic ideas, and science proves what religion discovered through faith, cooperation between disciplines rather than competition will become the rule rather than the exception. When reincarnation is accepted as a fact of life rather than a whimsical theory of New Age mystics, people will surely stop polluting the planet. They will help to create a better future world, knowing that they will return to it.

Past-life therapy

According to Dr Ian Stevenson, a psychiatrist who has devoted sixty years of his life to the study of and research into men and women who claim memory of other lives, we are on the brink of proving reincarnation to be an irrefutable truth. He said that during his initial years of research he did not believe that we return to this Earth again and again. He now says that the evidence that we do is too compelling for us to doubt it.

My individual counselling sessions always include regressions into other lives. Even people who doubt the validity of reincarnation have been surprised at the memories that come up which help them to release physical pain or ill health, heal relationships and understand themselves and others better. To re-live a past life is to relieve the emotion or trauma left over from it – although of course many past-life memories are happy. When I walk into a room I often see people dressed in the clothes of other lives, both past and future. It is as if these lives are occurring simultaneously, and so when we heal and change a negative aspect of one life, this automatically affects the others.

Past-life therapy exercises

Past-life therapy is already accepted today by many doctors and psychologists as a means of discovering the cause of a problem rather than treating its symptoms. Deep-seated problems are better sorted out with the help of a therapist. However, a simple way to begin is to sit comfortably, breathe and relax, and then imagine facing and going through in turn three doors. One is the door to the past, another to the present, and the third to the future.

Initially, in your mind's eye, compare all three, their shape, colour and size, and to which you feel most drawn to open first. Before going through the door to the past, you might ask to be shown either another life that may be impinging on the current one, or a time in this life that needs healing or resolving. Ask to be shown clearly what from the past of this or another life is affecting you today, what you need to focus more attention on or release altogether in the present, and what qualities from future or co-existent selves you can draw into your life today.

At the end, blend these images together, and merge with them, knowing that they will then become part of your soul's wisdom, and that their energy will co-operate with rather than fight against you.

A different way to get in touch with another life is to focus on a person, country, piece of music, literature or history, that for some reason feels familiar and comfortable. Having gone through the preliminary breathing and relaxation techniques, close your eyes and mentally say: 'Where did I know you before?' Concentrate on the person or place and keep repeating the question until the answer comes.

You can also do this with people and places you dislike and feel resistant to. Once you understand the source of a problem it no longer has power over you. You may even find dislike is replaced by peaceful acceptance once you understand the background cause.

The key to successful inner work is to let your creative imagination have free rein to play and practise. You might want to explore the life that has the greatest affect on your present one; or where a particular block came from; or your best and worst lives. If you do this, try and get in touch with how these lives ended. This is one way of overcoming the fear of death.

In my individual therapy sessions I now suggest to clients with whom I've worked before that they may like to explore life in other dimensions, on other planes and planets or try and discover co-existent, alternate personalities. These journeys can help us welcome the idea of ourselves as multi-dimensional beings instead of fearing it.

You might want to imagine drifting down into the past, floating through a blue mist which gradually clears, enabling you to see what is there. If you find that there is something unfinished, use your imagination to complete it, visualise a new outcome, heal, forgive or release the personality you discover. If it is yourself, integrate with it before opening your eyes.

Past lives and karma

As we begin to understand and clear old karma – what we have set in motion for ourselves from one life to another – we become more self-reliant and responsible. Karma is really a refining of ourselves. Each lifetime provides myriad experiences through which we can grow and learn, and for many this current life is one in which we can clear the karma of every other. In past epochs, we had time to deal with the results of what we created. As the planetary vibratory rate increases, we are dealing with instant manifestations or immediate karma. For example, my next-door neighbour, without permission, cut down a tree in our garden and was baffled by my reaction. About three hours later, another neighbour cut down one of the first neighbour's trees, and my first neighbour was outraged. This is instant karma.

Many of us today are reincarnating into another life without actually leaving our physical bodies. We sense the Wei Chi time of death and birth. It is the death of limitation and of the false identity, and a birth into a world vastly different from anything we have experienced before. A new baby cries a lot, sleeps a lot, and, away from the comfort and safety of his mother's womb, no doubt feels as if it has been thrown out of home before it is ready, and is vulnerable in what is initially an alien world. Many of us cry a lot, sleep a lot, and feel just as vulnerable, as we awaken to new life in this coming epoch. All the exercises that remind us that we have been here many times, played many parts, and do not have to carry the unnecessary baggage of our pasts around with us any more, help trigger our consciousness to leap into the unknown with excitement rather than fear.

Focusing on priorities

Visualisation is not the only way to heal ourselves, but is a road to expand our consciousness into higher dimensions, and literally helps us bridge the gap between our physical and spiritual senses. Aside from the myriad forms of inner work available to us, we can also help to bridge this gap by our style of life, one aspect of which is to allow ourselves time to do what we most love to do. Most of us are so busy trying to survive that we are not fully alive. We need to focus on our true priorities, simplify our lives, and drop what is unimportant.

There is a story of a monk who spent seventy years of his life trying to levitate to impress his Master. He finally flew across a lake and landed at his Master's feet, exclaiming: 'I can fly! I can fly!' The Master replied: 'Why did you waste so much time on levitation when you could easily have taken the boat?' What do *we* waste our time on which is not really necessary?

Detoxifying our bodies

We should get our priorities right as concerns our health and diet too. We can eat fresh, live food, lots of fruit, vegetables, nuts and pulses, rather than overload our bodies with the toxicity that comes from too much dead meat and processed food. Years ago, I became a vegetarian, and for two years lived entirely on raw food. I felt better and had more energy than at any other time in my life. I now eat fish and cooked vegetables, but still like to eat a lot of raw food. This diet may not suit everyone, but certainly improves my own lightness of being.

To clear the body of toxicity Drink at least eight glasses of water a day, and try to do an occasional three-day fast. If you feel that you will not survive on no food at all, do a three-day grape, apple or water-melon fast. This means eating the same food all the time, and no tea, coffee or alcohol. Alternatively, try a once-a-week fast, eating your lunch one day, then nothing until the evening of the next day. After fasting, especially for three days, your mind will feel crystal-clear and your body light, and the first food you eat will taste like the nectar of the gods.

Lymphatic cleansing exercise

1 Lie flat on your back, arms by your side, palms up, legs comfortably stretched. Keeping your head still, move your eyes as if trying to look behind your head. Take a long deep breath in, slowly raise your right arm up and

---

back over your shoulder. Stop 5 cm (2 inches) from the floor and hold for three seconds. With a long, deep breath out, slowly bring your arm back to its original position. Repeat with your left arm and then alternate arms for eight repeats. *

2 Look straight ahead. Take a long deep breath in, slowly raise your right leg up and over your shoulder. Stop 5 cm (2 inches) from the floor. Hold for three seconds. With a long breath out, slowly bend your knee to your chest. Feel the stretch as you raise your leg, sole facing the ceiling. Slowly return to your original position. Then alternate eight times with your left leg.

3 Sit on the floor, clasp your knees to your chest with your feet 15 cms (6 inches) apart. Keeping the legs still, take a deep breath in, rock back, stretching your arms as far as possible. With a deep breath out, rock forwards as far as possible. Repeat eight times.

4 Sit on a chair, feet shoulder-width apart with your hands palm down on your knees. Keep your eyes on your hands and slowly turn your right knee outwards until the foot begins to lift off the floor. Stop. Repeat eight times, alternating with your left knee.

5 Lie flat on your stomach, hands flat on the floor, 15 cms (6 inches) away from your ears. Take a deep breath in. Use your arms to raise the upper body, head back as far as possible. Lower to the floor with a deep breath out. Repeat eight times.

6 Get up. Take three deep breaths.

* Always alternate repeats and do same number of repeats on each side, or you will feel out of balance. This exercise is good for stress and digestion.

Breathing exercise

Beinsa Douna instructed his students to walk every day, preferably away from the smoke and dust of the city, and to practise breathing and physical exercises daily. Ten to fifteen minutes of the following exercise will improve the quality of our breathing as well as our attitude to the day.

Stand with your feet shoulders' width apart, slowly inhale and open your arms wide. Hold your breath, then slowly bring your arms forward and upwards, palms touching before exhaling. Repeat as many times as you can. Even if we can only do exercises in our own houses or apartments rather than outside, the benefits can be life-changing.

Greeting the sun

Beinsa Douna also taught his students to greet the sun at dawn and sunset, rather as did the Essenes. The Hopi Indians greet the morning sun with this prayer:

> I ask that this day
> The Sky Father and Earth Mother
> Meet in my heart,
> That they will be inseparable
> Today and for ever more. HO!

A new perspective

To go to the mountains or climb the nearest hill can also give us a new perspective in the same way as can meditation. Beinsa Douna said that one of the most helpful practices for a healthy life was to go to the mountains for as long as possible at least once a year. In this way our spirits can meet and greet spirits descending from above.

A harmonious environment

In Africa, a man I know built new houses for the workers on his father's farm. They were square bungalows with modern kitchens and bathrooms. With great excitement, the workers moved in. Six months later they all moved back to their round mud huts, saying that they were losing their souls in square houses and with tiled floors separating their feet from the ground. Black Elk made a similar statement about the native American Indians after the whites put them into square houses.

We may not all be able to live in round houses, but we can arrange our possessions in such a way that energy circulates smoothly, and people feel comfortable and revitalised. In the orient this 'art of placement' is called Feng Shui. Feng Shui takes years of study and practice. It is based on the recognition of the invisible energy flowing through all space and form, and how best to use it to create harmony.

In China, Feng Shui experts are often called in to advise on the exterior and interior design of new buildings, and harmoniously to realign the interiors of existing buildings, including homes, in order to bring good fortune to those working or living within them. Because this skilled and intuitive shaping of our surroundings can have so great an influence upon our health and happiness, it is certainly well worth our while to apply Feng Shui to our own lives.

The Chinese believe that if people work in surroundings that harm or stunt their chi, nothing will succeed. Chi, or Life Force, animates all things – trees, rivers, flowers – and without it human beings would not exist. Sarah Rossback, author of *Feng Shui* (pronounced 'Fung Schway'), says that Feng Shui experts are 'priests and doctors of environmental ills'. As priests they read and interpret visible and invisible signs and positive forces; as doctors they detect the Earth's pulse, analysing physical settings and determining how people can live and build without disturbing the Earth's energies, while also taking advantage of favourable energy flows. An example is that a stream running close to a house can disperse energy and carry away good fortune, whereas a pond, lake or river in front of a house bestows positive energy on its inhabitants.

To stimulate and amplify chi we must keep our houses sparkling clean and bright. Wind chimes, bells, crystals, crystal pendants that scatter rainbows around when hung in a window, water splashing from a fountain, mirrors, plants, flowers, light fresh colours – all help the flow of chi in our environment.

Alignment with the Tao

Feng Shui, which means 'wind-water', can help us live in alignment with the Tao. Alignment with the Tao means that everything falls into place for us, and life is no longer a constant battle. Inner and outer realms, conscious and unconscious, begin to work together. Jung's theory of synchronicity is in harmony with the Tao. For example, while writing this book, I could not locate the girl who agreed to type for me. After fifteen phone calls, I began to feel a little desperate. Suddenly the daughter of a friend appeared on my doorstep and asked if I had any typing to be done.

Again while preparing this book, I had just written a few words on Nostradamus when someone switched on the radio, and I heard, uncannily, almost word for word what I had just put down. On another occasion, I needed urgently to go shopping, but did not want to interrupt my work. Astoundingly, a friend walked into the kitchen with a huge basket of fruit and vegetables from a local farm. These synchronicities are happening more and more frequently for all of us.

George Bernard Shaw described the world we are rapidly moving into with these words: 'The visible world is not the only reality, and the invisible no longer a dream.' This blending of visible and invisible means that logic on its own does not work any more. If we try to do things in the old ways, there will either be no energy, or what we thought we ought to do will be interrupted by something totally different. We have to move from masculine to feminine, stop thinking, pushing, doing, and relax into feeling, listening, being and allowing. If we can do this the energy flows.

We who are of the twentieth to twenty-first century are crossing the boundaries between the known and unknown; there are no maps, there is no framework, we are moving into uncharted territory. We have to adapt to living in the middle of a hologram, where anything is possible, a quantum space of miracles and magic. We must remember that even if we do not consciously know how to take the next step the soul-essence of who we are contains the blueprint of what we came here to do and to be. We were born ready, with the answers within us. We have to start living from soul-essence, not just personality, from the intuition and inspiration of the heart, not of the mind.

The magic of living in the centre of a hologram, or to be aligned with the Tao, means that we do more by doing less. We picture and imagine every facet of what we want to accomplish first. If I write a book, I do not just sit down and start to type, but rather visualise for whom I am writing, and why; who will edit, print, publish and distribute this book; which country will the ink, trees and paper come from; who will cut the trees down, and so on.

From the centre of the hologram I create the whole picture, which allows the energy to flow, moves me into a different vibration, which draws to me everything I need to help this project without effort. This approach reminds us that we have inside us all the tools we need to accomplish or be whatever we want, that we can call on resources we have never called on before.

Visualising our own essence

To find and use our essence, we should simply imagine it forming at the top of our heads until it becomes so clear to our inner eye that we could almost touch it. Breathe it, through the chakras, into the solar plexus, and allow it to flow into whatever we want to do.

We have a responsibility to express ourselves, and the power to do so, as we have never had before. To understand what is happening now, we have to develop our spiritual senses, which may lead us to say: 'I do not understand, but I'm willing to create a space for the understanding to come in.' This is the difference between being and doing – it allows.

We may discover that our sole purpose in life is to express love. At the end of World War II a psychiatrist, entering a concentration camp to assess the health and psychological balance of the prisoners, met a man who was so radiantly healthy that he assumed him to be an informer, or recently captured. When questioned, the man said: 'I had the option to make the best or worst of the situation I was in. I decided to love everyone around me, captors and prisoners alike.'

By doing this, he not only affected everyone around him, but also himself. We can do the same today, by calling on our essence to hold everything and everyone around us in light. Simply picture them whole, healthy and happy. If we doubt our ability to make a difference, we can visualise drawing a sword of power from a rock, rather as King Arthur did with Excalibur. We must then claim the power that is rightfully ours and which is the sum total of all the experiences in all the lives that we have ever had.

Invoking the light of your love

The current universe cannot be understood rationally. Thinking about problems simply reinforces them. By opening our hearts, and using to the full the power of the imagination, we can catalyse enormous change.

Let us close our eyes for a moment, and imagine the flame of a candle inside our hearts. Let us feel it, imagine it getting bigger and bigger, and expanding to fill our entire bodies. The flame of our hearts reaches out, threads and streams of light, filigree threads of light, stream towards the members of our families, then into the hearts and minds of presidents and prime ministers, starving children in Africa and Bosnia, repressed people worldwide.

Imagine threads of light going out and out, connecting us with trees, flowers, the Earth, stones, hills, valleys, seas and lakes, with oceans, suns and moons. For a moment, let us be aware of life and light breathing us, not us breathing them. Let us breathe in joy and laughter, and let it out, breathe in sadness, sorrow, breathe it out. Imagine the whole planet suffused in the light of your love.

Awakening to change means that now the human heart can go the lengths of God. We have that power.

The human heart can go the lengths of God.
Dark and cold we may be, but this
Is no winter now. The frozen misery
Of centuries breaks, cracks, begins to move.
The thunder is the thunder of the floes,
The thaw, the flood, the upstart spring.
Thank God our time is now, when wrong
Comes up to face us everywhere,
Never to leave us till we take
The longest stride of soul men ever took.
Affairs are now soul size.
The enterprise is exploration into God.
Where are you making for? It takes
So many thousand years to wake,
But will you wake for pity's sake?

CHRISTOPHER FRY, *The Sleep of Prisoners*

13

TEACHINGS FOR A NEW AGE BEYOND THE NEXT MILLENNIUM

3001

A thousand years from now the human population will have been reduced to less than a billion, machines smaller than a pin head will be injected into people to clean their blood, everyone will be vegetarian, religion will be defunct and people will be able to 'manufacture' a human being.

These are some of the dramatic predictions of Arthur C. Clarke – scientist, futurologist and science-fiction author. In his book *3001: The Final Odyssey*, he describes a ring that floats high above the earth and encircles it. Hundreds of millions of people live in it, surrounded by lakes, plants and animals. There is no knowlege or skill that cannot be learned instantly – through caps that link their brains to Earth's databases they plug into centuries of history, science and entertainment. People greet each other by placing their palms together and swap, in a blink of an eye, information about one another that is contained within a microscopic chip placed under their skin at birth. Instead of spending time in gaol, law breakers are electronically monitored and subdued. (In Britain and America, tests on electronic tagging have already taken place.) Transport is driven by what he calls an 'inertialess drive', which acts on every molecule of a person's body, creating the effect of weightlessness. This allows people to cover vast distances at tens of thousands of kilometres an hour.

In 1945 Arthur C. Clarke invented the communications satellite. He predicted the arrival of the fax-machine and electronic mail. He is regarded as the brain behind the idea of using satellites for weather forecasting and the use of computers, although he did not expect them to be small enough to use in every home.

Today, microchips are already in use and scientists are working on a microchip which will use the body as part of an electronic network to exchange business card information or telephone numbers simply by shaking hands.

The ring around the Earth, and the massive towers that would connect the ring to it, are also scientifically possible. Clarke based his idea on Yuri Artsutanov's theories that it was possible to build a 'space-elevator', connecting Earth with a satellite in orbit. The difficulty would be finding material strong enough to do this, but in 1990 scientists discovered a third form of carbon which they say is the strongest material currently in existence and which would make the idea of 'space-elevators' possible.

New perspectives

While Arthur C. Clarke talks about a possible future in 3001, the Pleiadians, through channel Barbara Marciniak, tell us that we have a 'commitment to evolve in 3D'; that we must learn to handle many realities at once, balance many worlds at once. If this sounds complicated, remember how we already have to balance the different worlds and perceptions of body, mind, spirit and emotion. Each of these views reality in a different way. The Pleiadians say that, as we evolve today, we need to own our emotions and not deny them. 'The mutation occurring is the evolution or plugging-in of internal data to external data. The clearing occurring is the accessing of all the emotional bodies you have been frightened of using. You need to access your emotional body in order to understand your spiritual body. The mental body and physical body go hand in hand, while the spiritual and emotional bodies go hand in hand. Because the spiritual body is non-physical and you are locked into the physical realm, you must access the whole realm of the non-physical through your emotions.'

The Pleiadians say that we should focus on the energy centres of our body – our chakras – every day, as well as practise deep breathing and spinning similar to the Whirling Dervishes. Spinning is a way to align with the accelerated energy that now affects us, increasing our psychic perception and stimulating chakra activity.

Years before the Pleiadians began to communicate with humanity I, without conscious knowledge of what I did, used to spin anti-clockwise to disperse negative energy and clockwise to invoke light. I did this at least ten times in each direction and always felt free and light afterwards. I sometimes introduced this to seminar participants as I found that if it was done with the eyes half-closed, it introduced a slightly altered state of consciousness, which was useful for mandala drawing or visualisation exercises. At the end of crystal workshops I began to invite the group to split into an inner and outer circle; one circle walked clockwise, the other anti-clockwise. Each person held a crystal pointed horizontally left or right, at chest or heart level. The inner circle angled their crystals to the left, the outer circle to the right. As the two circles moved slowly around each other, and preferably to music, an almost palpable energy was generated – similar to the electricity produced by a generator. Each person felt stimulated, elated and free from the ties that appear to bind us to the earth.

I think that much of what the Pleiadians try to tell us is that we must learn to experience altered states of consciousness and different realities without fear.

From a totally different perspective, Robert Muller, who used to be Assistant Secretary General to the United Nations, says that, as we move towards the year 2000, we need a new cosmic spirituality, a new planetary management. He is worried about over-communication, leading to misinformation being spread around the world. In his words, 'We have to sit down with the firms and multi-nationals and place them in front of their responsibilities to the management of the planet ... we need world information, honest information and *not* manipulated information.' He talks about the need for world philanthropy to support global projects, ... simple, frugal lifestyles. 'We push people to buy more and more, but when we buy these things we tax the resources of the planet.'

Miller points out the need for a new world creativity and inspiration from artists and musicians. He says we are taught to love our neighbours and are then expected to kill them to defend land, an identity or an ideal. This cannot work. In Miller's words: 'cosmic education for children is needed ... we need to teach children a new art of living. It is their role to be the right managers of the planet tomorrow. We have to love humanity, the planet, the universe and our fragile years upon this planet. We are each of us a miracle and therefore cannot kill or hurt another miracle. We are cosmic units and we have the universe in ourselves and this has to be taught to the children so that they can flower to the responsibility for which they have been born.' He also suggests we need a new philosophy that allows us to realise that we are all instruments of God. (Or instruments of the universe, for those who do not believe in God.) 'Then we will have validated life and we will make people proud to be alive again.'

A major teacher for the now and future age is Dr Jim Hurtak, founder of The Academy for Future Science, and author of *The Book of Knowledge: The Keys of Enoch*. Jim Hurtak is a social scientist, a 'futurist' and researcher into remote sensing technology (or remote viewing, discussed in Chapter 6). He was the scientific consultant to Sydney Sheldon for his book *Doomsday Conspiracy*, as well as for numerous film and television documentaries. The *Keys of Enoch* is described as a 'blueprint of the many levels of spiritual consciousness and designed to bring us in touch with the meaning of Divine Intelligence'.

Hurtak says the keys of future knowledge mean essentially the keys to open terrestial and celestial doors together. He talks of humanity as being spiritual pilgrims who must work together, and extra-terrestial intelligences (with whom he has had contact) as having a 'fourth brain nodule that is a micro-crystalline extension of the brain's neurological wet-ware' to facilitate communication. Maybe this is a different description of the microchip that, according to Arthur C. Clarke, we will all be using in 3001.

In a recent interview Carlos Casteneda, who wrote many books around the teachings of Don Juan, and who describes himself as a sorcerer's apprentice, said that Don Juan considered himself a navigator of infinity and that in order to navigate into the unknown, as a shaman does, 'one needs unlimited pragmatism, boundless sobriety and guts of steel'. In other words, the goal of Don Juan's shamanism is to break the parameters of historical and everyday perception and to perceive the unknown. That is why he called himself a navigator of infinity, which lies beyond the parameters of daily perception. To break these parameters was the aim of his life

Carlos Casteneda has recently presented a physical discipline called 'Tensegrity', which consists of specific movements that promote health, vitality and a general sense of well-being. This reminds me of the Paneurhythmy taught by Beinsa Douna, which I learned in the mountains of Bulgaria. Paneurhythmy is a form of sacred, meditative dance to violin music which uses every muscle, limb and organ of the body. It is a life-changing exercise that creates a shift of awareness, merging inner and outer worlds. (For further information about Paneurhythmy see address at back of book.)

In 1931 a Japanese mystic, teacher and healer, Mokichi Okada, had a revelation that 1931 was the beginning of what is now called The New Age. Mokichi Okada – who later became known as Meishu Sama – had a revelation in which he was told the Earth was going to experience cataclysmic change in order to karmically balance and heal humanity's past mistakes. He also said that a similar upheaval would take place in the spiritual realms, as the world made its transition from darkness into light. Meishu Sama described the changes ahead as a time of world purification in order to remove pain and suffering and allow mankind to live as was originally intended, in peace, joy and prosperity.

Forces of change

When I worked as Paul Solomon's assistant, I remember a lecture he gave in London on 'Earth Changes'. He described earthquakes erupting under our feet, giant seas and tidal waves that would ultimately turn inland cities into seaside resorts, volcanic explosions that would spew out molten lava in some parts of the world, while in others an instant Ice Age would freeze us. Paul also said these cataclysmic geographical changes, from the weather to a new world landscape, with islands disappearing and others, such as Atlantis, reappearing were *our*, humanity's, fault. My mother and three aunts, who were amongst Paul's audience for the first time, were both furious and frightened. So much so they left before the end and did not hear him say that a prophecy that comes true is a prophecy that has failed. Predicted destiny is influenced by human will and consciousness; therefore the purpose of a prophecy is to give us ample opportunity to change.

Faced with so many predictions of forthcoming disasters, combined with numerous messages of love, light and support from inter-galactic beings, who are bombarding the planet with spiritual energy to assist the earth's transition into a new form, what can we ourselves do on our own? How can we each bring about personal, global and cosmic transformation?

Remember too that what we do on our own affects everything and everybody around us. It is the hundredth Monkey Syndrome which recognises that our behaviour and beliefs are influenced by the collective unconscious. Ken Keyes said, 'When a certain critical number achieves an awareness, this new awareness may be communicated directly mind to mind. There is a point at which, if only one more person tunes into a new awareness, a field is strengthened so that this awareness is picked up by almost everyone.'

In St John's *Revelation* he describes a scroll with seven seals and how, when each one is opened, a different energy is released. The first four to be opened release the well known horsemen of the apocalypse: death, war, famine and pestilence – all of which we face today. The seals are an allegorical reference to the human chakra system. As new energies hit us, our chakras react to the stimulation and we need to master/overcome the challenges relative to the qualities of each one. This is why it is increasingly important to understand our chakra system. In addition this allows us to be far more tolerant and accepting of others. If, for example, I know that my child is currently more focused on his third chakra, while my husband is expressing himself from the fifth, and I am on the fourth, I will understand that we all have a slightly different perspective. I will make allowances for it, rather than blame or criticise.

Transformation

I mentioned earlier that part of the planetary transformation we are currently undergoing is a shift from duality to unity. This means we must stop judging people or situations as good or bad, black or white. If we resist or judge what appears to be evil or fearful, we give it power. Jesus said: 'Love your enemies,' and when we can do this we empower ourselves.

As we begin to communicate telepathically and, with heightened senses, see both visible and invisible worlds, we will also see that the human tendency to polarise, or separate and compartmentalise everything, is ridiculous because ultimately all is one. We must release others to their own experience, while we may discern that particular experience is not our choice at this time.

Judgement, hate, criticism, fear and lack of forgiveness for ourselves and others are ways to weaken ourselves and our lives. To move easily between dimensions, adjust to new wavelengths, requires love. Without love we cannot do it.

The current changes are multifaceted. Many things are taking place in our lives simultaneously – both internally and externally. To cope, we need to continually remember that all of life is energy and vibration. If we keep our own vibratory fields or wavelengths at high levels, we will move through the Earth's transition with ease.

We can compare ourselves to an electric fan which, when not plugged in or activated, is just a lump of metal. Once switched on, the blades become invisible, but we can feel their effect. And if our fingers accidentally touched them, we'd be seriously hurt. In the same way, fast spinning vibrational fields, invisible to the naked eye, deflect negativity – and harm – away from us.

Homeopathy, bio-active vibrational healing, flower remedies such as those developed by Edward Bach, the South African gem and flower elixirs, the Australian bush essences, amongst many others, not only keep our vibrations up but also catalyse both self and spiritual awareness. Flower gem elixirs remove blocks which inhibit the free flow of energy in our physical and subtle bodies. Sun worship, crystals, bathing in the sea, streams or in pure spring water, all boost our immune system and revitalise our inner and outer selves.

Aura-Soma is a magical means of cleansing and clearing the electro-magnetic field around us as well as stimulating soul connection. Chimes, drums, singing bowls, chanting, and various wood instruments, all contribute to humanity's shift of consciousness.

How can we best align ourselves with the accelerated and higher frequencies of light that now affect life on planet Earth? How should we prepare ourselves for the new millennium? I believe the answer lies in the following:

1 Love. Unconditional love of self and others is the prerequisite for physical, mental, emotional and spiritual well-being.

2 Truth. Live what is true for you without apology or explanation. (I am not talking about cruelty or unkindness but to apologise and explain too much gives your power away.) Live what is true for your spiritual self, your heart-feeling self.

3 The Higher Soul or Godself. Make conscious contact with this aspect of your being. It perceives life from a very

different view to the physical and knows exactly how you may best live your life. It knows where you came from and where you are going to. It is a source of wisdom, information and love. Meditation, dreams, prayers, as well as the multitude of exercises available in this and other books can all help this communication.

4 Purify your physical body, your mind and feelings, in order to open fully to the spiritual realms.

5 Visualise the new world into existence and behave as if it is already here.

6 Celebrate life. Laugh. Enjoy yourself. In this way you will become a planetary healer, sparking joy in everyone and everything around you.

7 Part of celebrating life is to do what makes you feel happy. For example, wear clothes and colours you like. Do not save your best clothes, china, glass, linen etc . . ., for best. Use them today. Do not have anything around you that does not mean something to you or that gives you a buzz.

8 Use willpower to create the life you want. An example of this is the story of Ben & Jerry's ice-cream. Unemployed in the 1970s, they did a mail-order ice-cream making course and then started a business in Vermont, USA. Ben and Jerry's three main aims were to produce the best ice-cream, have a good return for shareholders and improve the quality of life for the local community. One way in which they did this was to use Brazilian nuts gathered from the rainforests to make Rainforest Crunch Ice-Cream. As a result they created an economy in Brazil which was not based on deforestation. The brownies, for their Fudge Brownie Ice-Cream, are made by the mentally ill or ex-drug addicts who are trying to establish a new life. They simply stopped complaining about how tough life was, got on their feet and got on.

9 Don't take any of the disaster predictions too seriously. Maybe they will happen, maybe not. Use your common sense and sense of humour. True spirituality is light,

sparkling, joyous and humorous – it is not heavy ritual or rules and regulations.

10 Remember that if we all take responsibility for our own lives, creativity and the Earth around us, we might even see a little bit of heaven on Earth before the millennium.

In the words of the 'Mother' who was part of Sri Aurobindo's Ashram in India: 'I invite you to the Great Adventure, and on this adventure you are not to repeat spiritually what others have done before, because our new adventure begins from beyond that stage. We are now for a new creation, entirely new, carrying in it all the unforeseen, all risks, all hazards – a new adventure – of which the way is unknown and has to be traced step out of step in the unexplored. It is something that has never been in the present universe and will never be in the same manner. If that interests you, well, embark.'

To embark on this great adventure requires us to move from our heads to our hearts, to live from the wisdom of our souls and not merely from our minds and personalities. It means we must drop our egos, shed any illusions we have about ourselves, others and life.

Two of the most inspirational figures of the 20th century who exemplify these words were Diana, Princess of Wales, self-crowned Queen of Hearts, and Mother Teresa, often dubbed 'Saint of the Slums'. Each in her own way became an archetypal image of love, courage, compassion, caring and kindness.

The lives of Princess Diana and Mother Teresa show that two single people *can* change the world and unite everyone in it into a global family. This was forcibly demonstrated by the extraordinary outpouring of grief at Princess Diana's death and funeral. The minute of silence, in which millions of people participated worldwide, was a spiritual event which signified a global awakening of the human heart and a turning point in the history of mankind.

We must now use the examples set by these two powerful and courageous women and ask ourselves: 'How can I change my life into something meaningful? How can I bring love and joy into desperately sad situations? What small deeds of kindness can I perform that make a difference? How can I break the barriers between myself and others?' If each of us achieved only one of these aims we would change the world. We do not need high-powered training to do so.

The Desiderata

Go placidly amid the noise and haste, and remember what peace there may be in silence. As far as possible without surrender be on good terms with all persons. Speak your truth quietly and clearly; and listen to others, even the dull and ignorant; they too have their story. Avoid loud and aggressive persons, they are vexations to the spirit. If you compare yourself with others, you may become vain and bitter; for always there will be greater and lesser persons than yourself. Enjoy your achievements as well as your plans. Keep interested in your own career, however humble; it is a real possession in the changing fortunes of time. Exercise caution in your business affairs; for the world is full of trickery. But let this not blind you to what virtue there is; many persons strive for high ideals and everywhere life is full of heroism. Be yourself. Especially, do not feign affection. Neither be cynical about love; for in the face of all aridity and disenchantment it is perennial as the grass. Take kindly the counsel of the years, gracefully surrendering the things of youth. Nurture strength of spirit to shield you in sudden misfortune. But do not distress yourself with imaginings. Many fears are born of fatigue and loneliness. Beyond a wholesome discipline, be gentle with yourself. You are a child of the Universe, no less than the trees and the stars; you have a right to be here. And whether or not it is clear to you, no doubt the Universe is unfolding as it should. Therefore be at peace with God, whatever you conceive him to be, and whatever your labours and aspirations, in the noisy confusion of life keep peace with your soul. With all its sham, drudgery and broken dreams, it is still a beautiful world. Be careful, strive to be happy.

FURTHER READING

Alder, Vera Stanley, *Finding the Third Eye, The Atomic Age, The 5th Dimension* (Rider)

Bach, Richard, *Illusions, Jonathan Livingston Seagull, One, The Gift of Living* (Pan)

Bailey, Alice, *Esoteric Astrology I & II, Esoteric Healing, Esoteric Psychology I & II, Glamour: A World Problem, Initiation: Human and Solar, The 7 Rays, Treatis on White Magic, Unfinished Biography* (Lucis Trust)

Bauval, Robert and Hancock, Graham, *Keepers of Genesis* (Mandarin)

Borysenko, Joan and Miroslav, *The Power of the Mind to Heal* (Eden Grove)

Brinkley, Dannion, *At Peace In The Light* and *Saved By The Light* (both Piatkus)

Brunton, Paul, *A Search in Secret India, A Secret Path, Secret Search in Egypt, The Hidden Teachings Beyond Yoga* (Rider)

Burhnam, Sophy, *Angels Letters; A Book of Angels* (Rider)

Campbell, Joseph, *Myths to Live By, The Masks of God* (Penguin)

Cayce, Edgar, *Edgar Cayce on Atlantis, Edgar Cayce on Reincarnation, Edgar Cayce's Story of Jesus, Edgar Cayce's Story of Karma* (Bantam)

Carey, Ken, *Vision* (Starseed)

Chopra, Deepak, *The Seven Spiritual Laws of Success* (Rider) (and all his other books)

Colton, Ann Ree, *Watch Your Dreams* (ARC)

Credo Mutwa, Vusamazulu, *Song of the Stars: The Lore of a Zulu Shaman* (Station Hill Openings Barrytown Ltd.)

Dalichow, Irene, and Booth, Mike, *Aura-Soma: Healing through Colour, Plant and Crystal Energy* (Hay House)

de Vries, Jan, *Viruses, Allergies and the Immune System* (and all his other books) (Mainstream Publishing)

Diamond, Harvey and Marilyn, *Fit for Life* (Bantam)

Dossy, Larry, *Healing Words: The Practice of Medicine* (HarperCollins)

Fortune, Dion, *Sane Occultism* (Aquarian)
Furth, Fred M., *The Secret World of Drawings: Healing through Art* (Siggo Press)
Gawain, Shakti, *Creative Visualisation* (Bantam)
Gill, Derek, *Quest: the Life of Elizabeth Kubler-Ross* (Harper & Row)
Giovetti, Paola, *Angels* (Weiser)
Girardet, Herbert, *Gaia Atlas of Cities* (Gaia)
Gurdjieff, *Views from the Real World* (Arkana)
Haiche, Elizabeth, *Initiation* (George Allen and Unwin)
Halifax, Joan, *Shamanic Voices* (Penguin)
Hay, Louise, *You Can Heal Your Life* (and all her other books) (Eden Grove Editions)
Hills, Christopher, *Nuclear Evolution: Discovery of Rainbow Body* (Centre Community Publications)
Jeffers, Susan, *End the Struggle and Dance with Life* (Coronet)
Jung, Carl, *Man and His Symbols* (Pan), *Memories, Dreams and Reflections* (Fontana)
Keating, Thomas, *Staying Well with Guided Imagery; Open Mind, Open Heart* (Element)
Keller, Thomas, and Taylor, Deborah S., *Angels* (Hampton Roads Publishing, US)
Kubler-Ross, Elizabeth, *On Death and Dying; Living with Death and Dying; Death – the Final Stage of Growth; Questions and Answers on Death and Dying* (Tavistock, Routledge, Souvenir Press, Prentice Hall)
Lerner, Michael, *Choices in Healing: the Best of Conventional and Complementary Approaches to Cancer* (MIT Press)
Maclean, Dorothy, *To Hear the Angels Sing* (Findhorn Press)
Meadows, Kenneth, *Where Eagles Fly* (Element)
Montgomery, Ruth, *A Search for the Truth* (Fawcett), *A World Beyond* (Futura) *Born to Heal* (J. K. Hall)
Moody, Raymond, *Reunions: Visionary Encounters with Departed Loved Ones* (Warner)
Moolenburgh, H. C., *A Handbook of Angels; Meetings with Angels* (C. W. Daniel)
Moore, Thomas, *Care of the Soul* (Piatkus Books)
Mynne, Hugh, *The Faerie Way* (Llewellyn Publications)
Newhouse, Flower, *The Kingdom of the Shining Ones* (Simon & Schuster)
Ostrander, Sheila, and Schroeder, Lynn, *Cosmic Memory* (Simon & Schuster)
Ouspensky & Schroeder, *A New Model of the Universe, In Search of the Miraculous, Tertium Organum, The Fourth Way* (Arkana)
Rinpoche, Sogyal, *The Tibetan Book of Living and Dying* (Rider)
Rossbach, Sarah, *Feng Shui* (Rider)
Snell, Joy, *The Ministry of Angels* (Christian Spiritualist Association)
Spalding, Baird T., *Life and Teachings of the Masters of the Far East* (Devorss)

FURTHER READING

Spangler, David, *A Pilgrim in Aquarius* (Findhorn Press)
Szekely, Edmond Bordeaux, *The Gospel of the Essnes* (C. W. Daniel)
Taylor, Terry Lynn, *Answers from the Angels; Messengers of Light* (H. J. Kramer)
Timms, Moira, *Prophecies to Take You into the Twenty-First Century* (Thorsons)
Uyldert, Mellie, *The Psychic Garden* (Thorsons)
Watson, Lyall, *The Romeo Error, Supernature* (Hodder and Stoughton)
Watts, Alan, *The Wisdom of Insecurity* (Rider)
Wilson, Colin, *The Occult: A History* (Hodder and Stoughton)
Yogananda, *Autobiography of a Yogi* (Rider)
Young, Meredith L., *Agartha: a Course in Cosmic Awareness* (Gateway Books)

Useful Addresses

Roy Gillett
32 Glynswood
Camberley
Surrey GU15 1HU

Hundredth Monkeying
16 Chilkwell Street
Glastonbury
Somerset BA6 6DB
Tel/Fax: (44) 01458 834576

Paneurhythmy
Danielle Carr-Gomm
258 Kew Road
Richmond
Surrey TW9 3EG
Tapes also available

Paul Panos
P.O. Box 171
McGregor 6708
South Africa
Tel/Fax: (2021) 23 27 87
Email: ptp@iafrica.com.

Petra Du Preez
P.O. Box 5123
Cape Town 8000
South Africa
Tel/Fax: (021) 23 27 87
Email: astrozon@iafrica.com.

For Robert Bly and Marion Woodman films contact:

Applewood Centre
Box 148
Ontario
Canada K8N 5AZ
Tel: 1 800 361 0541

For Soozi Holbeche workshops contact:

Maggie Roberts
260 Kew Road
Richmond
Surrey TW9 3EQ

For Soozi Holbeche or Paul Solomon tapes contact:

P.O. Box 23
Yateley
Camberley
Surrey GU17 7DW

INDEX

INDEX

Piatkus Books

If you have enjoyed reading this book, you may be interested in other titles published by Piatkus. These include:

Afterlife, The: An investigation into the mysteries of life after death Jenny Randles and Peter Hough

Ancient Egypt David P. Silverman

Ambika's Guide To Healing And Wholeness: The energetic path to the chakras and colour Ambika Wauters

Art As Medicine: Creating a therapy of the imagination Shaun McNiff

As I See It: A psychic's guide to developing your healing and sensing abilities Betty F. Balcombe

Ask Your Angels: A practical guide to working with angels to enrich your life Alma Daniel, Timothy Wyllie and Andrew Ramer

At Peace In The Light: A man who died twice reveals amazing insights into life, death and its mysteries Dannion Brinkley with Paul Perry

Beyond Belief: How to develop mystical consciousness and discover the God within Peter Spink

Care Of The Soul: How to add depth and meaning to your everyday life Thomas Moore

Channelling For Everyone: A safe, step-by-step guide to developing your intuition and psychic abilities Tony Neate

Child Of Eternity, A: An extraordinary young girl's message from the world beyond Adriana Rocha and Kristi Jorde

Children And The Spirit World: A book for bereaved families Linda Williamson

Chinese Face And Hand Reading Joanne O'Brien

Colour Your Life: Discover your true personality through colour reflection reading Howard and Dorothy Sun

Companion To Grief: Finding consolation when someone you love has died Patricia Kelly

Complete Book Of UFOs, The: An investigation into alien contacts and encounters Peter Hough and Jenny Randles

Journeys Through Time: A guide to reincarnation and your immortal soul Soozi Holbeche

Karma And Reincarnation: The key to spiritual evolution and enlightenment Dr Hiroshi Motoyama

Keys To The Temple, The: Unravel the mysteries of the ancient world David Furlong

Lao Tzu's Tao Te Ching Timothy Freke

Life After Death: Investigating heaven and the spiritual dimension Jenny Randles and Peter Hough

Life Signs: An astrological guide to the way we live Julia and Derek Parker

Light Up Your Life: And discover your true purpose and potential Diana Cooper

Living Magically: A new vision of reality Gill Edwards

Many Lives, Many Masters: The true story of a prominent psychiatrist, his young patient and the past-life therapy that changed both of their lives Dr Brian L. Weiss

Mary's Message To The World Annie Kirkwood

Meditation For Every Day: Includes over 100 inspiring meditations for busy people Bill Anderton

Meditation For Inner Peace Eddie and Debbie Shapiro

Meditation Kit, The: The complete starter pack for meditation and visualisation Charla Devereux and Fran Stockel

Message Of Love, A: A channelled guide to our future Ruth White

Messenger, The: The journey of a spiritual teacher Geoff Boltwood

Mindfulness Meditation For Everyday Life Jon Kabat-Zinn

Miracles: A collection of true stories which prove that miracles do happen Cassandra Eason

Only Love Is Real: A story of soulmates reunited Dr Brian L. Weiss

Paranormal Source Book, The: The comprehensive guide to strange phenomena worldwide Jenny Randles

Parting Visions: An exploration of predeath psychic and spiritual experiences Dr Melvin Morse with Paul Perry

Past Lives, Present Dreams: How to use reincarnation for personal growth Denise Linn

Time For Healing, A: The journey to wholeness Eddie and Debbie Shapiro
Time For Transformation, A: How to awaken to your soul's purpose and claim your power Diana Cooper
Toward A Meaningful Life: The wisdom of the Rebbe Menachem Mendel Schneerson Simon Jacobsen (ed.)
Transformed By The Light: The powerful effect of near-death experiences on people's lives Dr Melvin Morse with Paul Perry
Transform Your Life: A step-by-step programme for change Diana Cooper
Visualisation: An introductory guide Helen Graham
Working With Guides And Angels Ruth White
Working With Your Chakras Ruth White
World Mythology: The illustrated guide Dr Roy Willis
Yesterday's Children: The extraordinary search for my past-life family Jenny Cockell
Your Healing Power: A comprehensive guide to channelling your healing abilities Jack Angelo
Your Heart's Desire: Using the laws of manifestation to create the life you really want Sonia Choquette

For a free brochure with information on our full range of titles, please write to:

Piatkus Books
Freepost 7 (WD 4505)
London W1E 4EZ

PIATKUS